# READ ON
## CANADA

**PAUL SHARPLES • JUDITH CLARK**

Prentice Hall Regents Canada
Scarborough, Ontario

**Canadian Cataloguing in Publication Data**

Sharples, Paul, 1957–
    Read on Canada

ISBN 0-13-436510-0

1. English language — Textbooks for second language learners.* I. Clark, Judith, 1953–

II. Title.

PE1128.S53  1994     428.2'4     C94-932695-X

© 1995 Prentice-Hall Canada Inc., Scarborough, Ontario

ALL RIGHTS RESERVED
No part of the material protected by this copyright notice may be reproduced or utilized in any form or by any means, electronic or mechanical, including photocopying, recording, or by an information storage and retrieval system, without the written permission of the copyright owner.

Prentice-Hall, Inc., Englewood Cliffs, New Jersey
Prentice-Hall International (UK) Limited, London
Prentice-Hall of Australia, Pty. Limited, Sydney
Prentice-Hall Hispanoamericana, S.A., Mexico City
Prentice-Hall of India Private Limited, New Delhi
Prentice-Hall of Japan, Inc., Tokyo
Simon & Schuster Asia Private Limited, Singapore

Editora Prentice-Hall do Brasil, Ltda., Rio de Janeiro

ISBN 0-13-436510-0

Executive Editor: Cliff Newman
Managing Editor: Marta Tomins
Copy Editor: Mia London
Production Editor: Imogen Brian
Production Coordinator: Anna Orodi
Cover Design: Julie Fletcher
Interior Design and Page Layout: VISU*TronX* – J. Loates/Linda Deramaix

1 2 3 4 5 W 99 98 97 96 95

Printed and bound in Canada

Every reasonable effort has been made to obtain permissions for all articles and data used in this edition. If errors or omissions have occurred, they will be corrected in future editions provided written notification has been received by the publisher.

This book is printed on recycled paper.

# Table of Contents

## Introduction     v
    To the Student

    To the Teacher

## Chapter I—Sun, Sea, Wind, and Sky
    1. Canada's Endangered Wilderness     3

    2. Just Another Load of Garbage?     11

    3. Saving the World by Cycling     21

## Chapter II—Toward a Healthier Canada
    1. Dr. Peter: AIDS Educator     31

    2. Of Shamans, Plants, and Healing     40

    3. The Sounds of Silence     46

## Chapter III—Taking Action Against Crime
    1. High Tech Crime Fighting     55

    2. These Hackers Don't Play Golf     61

    3. Building Community Partnerships     68

## Chapter IV—Protecting and Providing
    1. Wronged and Rights     81

    2. In Service of Others     88

    3. Consumers Protected     96

## Chapter V—Canada in the Global Village
    1. The Reconciliation: Canada's UN Peacekeepers     106

    2. Helping People To Help Themselves: OXFAM-Canada     113

    3. Getting Away With Murder     121

## Notes     130

# Introduction

## To the Student

Canada is a wonderful, exciting, and complex nation. The purpose of this book is to introduce you to some of the most important social and cultural issues facing Canadians today. You will be encouraged to explore these issues with your classmates and to put your thoughts into writing.

To acquire new language skills, you will work with partners, with small groups, and with the whole class. You may also go out into the community to find out more about aspects of Canadian society that make us proud and that help give our lives purpose and direction.

You will be encouraged to take risks—and even to make mistakes!—as you continue to develop your communication skills. Learning a new language is a tremendous challenge and you are well on your way to meeting that challenge. We hope that this book will, in many different ways, inspire you to take pride in your accomplishments and to become caring and aware participants in Canadian society.

## To the Teacher

*Read On Canada* is a reader for intermediate to upper-level students of English as a second or additional language. It is recommended for use in high school, college, university, or community ESL programs. It employs a content-based approach to language learning and is based on the assumption that students will improve their reading skills only if the content excites them and if they are reading for authentic purposes. It requires a supportive, flexible, and creative language learning environment.

At this level of language acquisition, some of the pride and excitement of the "beginner" has worn thin. Students have become more aware of the complexities of mastering English. Their efforts may bring less satisfaction and progress, fewer rewards. This text is designed to create a renewed sense of achievement for students as they engage in meaningful activities about topics relevant to their new lives in Canada.

Each of the fifteen articles focuses on an important social or cultural issue facing Canadians today. Because our students come from a variety of cultural, ethnic, and educational backgrounds, topics reflect a broad range of human experience. Although Canadian in focus, each unit provides students with opportunities to examine issues from personal, regional, and international perspectives.

# Text Format

## I. Pre-Reading Activities

### A. Before You Read

Research has shown that the reader's background knowledge is the most powerful determinant of comprehension.[1] The questions in this section are designed to activate prior knowledge and link this knowledge to the new information provided.

Students are asked to predict what they think an article will be about. Write a sampling of their predictions on the board. In this way, students begin to set their own purposes for reading.

## B. A Reminder to Use Context Clues

Good readers predict, hypothesize, and monitor ideas as they actively build meaning. Many English-as-a-second-language students need to be weaned from their translating dictionaries.

Assure students that many potentially unfamiliar words are explained by the article itself. Alert students to the following five methods used to define "new" words in the text. All examples are from the first article, "Canada's Endangered Wilderness."

**Direct definition:** A wilderness area is an unchanging stretch of land where humans have had little influence or control.

**Restatement:** Establishing protected wilderness areas, or reserves, is not enough.

**Example:** Wetlands, forests, and even a small pond are all examples of ecosystems. (Students must be willing to guess what the items have in common before concluding what a term means.)

**Inference:** We must also protect wildlife from poachers who illegally trap or kill animals.

**Contrast:** However, when we turn forests into farms and cities, or when we dig mines and drain wetlands, we are not helping keep ecosystems balanced.

In addition to working on direct and inferred definitions, students may need instruction on how to identify and interpret transition signals and linking words. The following words and phrases are examples of the signal words used in this text.

**Sequence:** first, second, next, finally, last

**Addition**: and, also, as well, another, first of all, furthermore, in addition, similarly, moreover

**Change of direction:** but, however, in contrast, nevertheless, on the other hand, otherwise, still, yet, in spite of, despite, even though, although

**Explanation:** for example, for instance, such as, that is, in other words

**Emphasis:** indeed, in fact, above all, most of all, remember that, central issue, in short

**Causation:** for, because, since, as, due to

**Consequence:** so, therefore, consequently, as a result

**Conclusion:** finally, in conclusion, in summary, last

# II. Responding to the Article

## A. Journal Writing and Discussion

Journal activities provide students with the opportunity to begin to make personal sense out of the information provided. Encourage students to write without fear of the red pen. The primary audience is the writer, then his or her classmates, and finally the teacher. Encourage students to share their responses in groups of three to four members.

It is recommended that students have a separate journal section in their notebook. This will give students a sense of continuity and progression as they complete their journal writing activities throughout the term.

## B. Finding the Main Ideas

Students remain in groups to discuss the main ideas of the article they have just read. They will probably need some assurance that they do not need to understand every word in order to understand the main ideas. Most of the main ideas in the articles are explicit and they are typically located at the beginning of paragraphs.

If students require additional instruction about topic and supporting sentences in a paragraph, you might try the following activity.

Choose a sample paragraph. Cut the paragraph apart line by line and put each slip in an envelope. Instruct groups of students to organize the slips into a well-written paragraph. Compare results between groups, and between the newly assembled paragraph and the original. Students will soon see the connection between topic sentences and main ideas.

# III. Comprehension Check

## A. Questions: Parts I and II

Encourage students to continue working in their groups to respond to and write questions about the information presented.

Both literal and inferential questions are provided to guide students in reviewing and evaluating the information provided.

When students are writing their own questions, they should be required to include some "why" and "how" questions that cover more than the details and facts often targeted by the "who," "what," "when," and "where" questions.

Passing along one group's questions to another group gives this exercise an authentic audience.

## B. True, False, and INP (Information Not Provided)

Students work in partners to complete these exercises. Students will need to reread and review specific sections of the article to support their choices. Once completed, students may take turns "being teacher" by leading a whole-class discussion.

# IV. Word Power

This section includes a variety of vocabulary-building exercises: definitions, synonyms, antonyms, cloze exercises, and word form choices.

Once again, encourage students to work with a partner in order to give these exercises a communicative purpose. Vocabulary acquisition is a complex process, and students are best able to learn a word when they feel a personal need for that word. Working together, students will want to do their part to contribute to the partnership.

# V. Active Interaction

The interaction activities provide further opportunities for students to work cooperatively in small groups on tasks that build on the concepts developed in the reading. Students will use language for a variety of authentic purposes including surveys, role plays, problem solving, decision making, and interviews.

## VI. Further Topics for Discussion and Composition

These oral and written activities have been included to help students learn and think critically about the content provided. Recent research clearly indicates that the development of writing skills enhances the development of reading skills.

Students may work alone, in pairs, or in small groups to respond to these questions and suggestions. This is an opportunity for teachers to choose and distribute assignments to suit the individual needs of the students.

The possibilities for extension activities linked to the topics introduced in these articles are limited only by your own creativity and the enthusiasm of the class. In addition, organizations such as the Sierra Club, Western Canada Wilderness Society, OXFAM, Amnesty International, and others have developed extensive school-based programs.

## VII. Journal Writing

Students go back to their journals and log what they have learned and experienced after each particular unit of study.

Many students may feel frustrated by their lack of facility with English to express adequately the complexity of the concepts learned, and teachers may consider allowing students to complete this assignment in their first language.

Asking students to use their first language shows them that their first languages are valued and gives them the opportunity to further develop academic proficiency in that language. Many researchers, such as Cummins in his "Developmental Interdependence Hypothesis," point to competence in the second language as a function of competence in the first language.[2]

## VIII. Unit Crossword Puzzles

When students complete a puzzle, their success shows them that they are making progress and that they are able to recall and use the vocabulary learned.

# Suggestions for Getting Started

## I. Preview the Text Together
- Look at the title. What could it mean?
- Skim the Table of Contents. Is it chronological or conceptual?
- Look at the format of the articles and activities. Are they consistent?
- List the kinds of visuals used: photographs, graphs, charts, maps. Do you know how to read them?
- Notes. Where are they and what is their purpose?

## II. Model Successful Reading Strategies

Try a teacher "think-aloud." Read through the first article paragraph by paragraph and "think aloud" your own strategies for reading the selection. Show students how to guess at meanings using context clues and signal words. Comment as the main ideas of the article become clearer to you.

**Have fun!**

*Mountain climbing in the Pantheon Range, British Columbia*
T. Daum

# Chapter I

# SUN, SEA, WIND, AND SKY

Read On Canada

*Young volunteers feed the ducks at Reifel Bird Sanctuary in Delta, B.C.*
Paul Sharples

*Cross-country skiing near Pemberton, British Columbia*
Evelyn Feller

*Sun, Sea, Wind, and Sky*

# Canada's Endangered Wilderness

## I. Pre-Reading Activities

### A. Before You Read

Before reading the article, complete the following activities with the rest of the class.

- What do you think the author will say about our relationship to the earth?
- What does the word "wilderness" mean?
- Look at the bottom photograph on page 2.
- Have you ever visited any wilderness areas, either in Canada or in your native country?
- Tell the rest of your class about your visit(s).
- Many of these areas in Canada are disappearing. What do you think are some of the reasons for this?
- What do you think you will learn about in this article?

Go ahead and read the article. Try to guess the meaning of words that you do not know.

1  Canada is a country made up of many different kinds of wilderness areas. A wilderness area is an unchanging stretch of land where we have had little influence or control. These areas include, for example, the ancient rain forests of British Columbia, the tallgrass and wetlands of the prairies, the vast Arctic tundra, and the Maritime coasts. Wilderness areas are home to over 70 000 known species of plants and animals.[1] They provide most of our fresh drinking water. They contain medicines that help us fight diseases such as cancer, and they have been an inspiration to painters, writers, and musicians for thousands of years.

2  Unfortunately, much of Canada's wilderness is rapidly disappearing. Many of our rivers and lakes are being polluted by harmful chemicals from cars, factories, and power plants.[2] We cut down our ancient rain forests and sell the wood all over the world. We turn our tallgrass prairie into agricultural land to grow food. To make room for cities and highways, we drain the Great Lake wetlands. We also damage wilderness areas in the Yukon and Northwest Territories when we dig for minerals such as nickel and gold.[3]

*Prairie tallgrass: only about one percent remains unaffected.*
Courtesy of the Critical Wildlife Habitat Program, Winnipeg, Manitoba

*A clearcut near the head waters of the Escalante River on the west coast of Vancouver Island.*
Ivona Sindlerova

3   When we damage or destroy a wilderness area, we lose more than just beautiful scenery. We also lose ecosystems. Wetlands, forests, and even a small pond are examples of ecosystems. In ecosystems, plants and animals live together with their surroundings and depend upon each other for survival. Some species provide shelter to others. In a forest ecosystem, a dead tree might provide a home for a bird. One type of species might provide food for another. Trees make their food from the sun and nutrients in the soil. A chipmunk eats the seeds of the tree and a larger animal eats the chipmunk. By working together, plants and animals help keep ecosystems balanced.

4   However, when we turn forests into farms and cities, or when we dig mines and drain wetlands, we are not helping keep ecosystems balanced. These changes can make it difficult for a species to survive. Already in Canada nine species of plants and animals have died out and become extinct over the past 200 years.[4] In addition, the Committee on the Status of Endangered Wildlife in Canada estimates that 278 species are now at risk.[5] At risk means in danger of eventual extinction. If we continue to destroy our wilderness areas at our current speed, all wilderness that exists outside of parks or wilderness reserves will be gone within the next 30 years.[6]

5 Environmental groups such as the World Wildlife Fund and the Canadian Parks and Wilderness Society (CPAWS), along with more than 90 other conservation organizations, are working with the federal, provincial, and territorial governments to have at least 12 percent of Canada protected as parks and wilderness reserves by the year 2000.[7] So far, only about 3.4 percent of Canada is protected from forestry, mining, and other resource development.[8]

6 Establishing protected wilderness areas, or reserves, is not enough, however. We must teach people who visit these areas to take care of them. Garbage that hikers and campers leave behind, especially metal and plastic packaging, can injure or kill wildlife that tries to eat it. Unwatched campfires and careless smoking can cause forest fires. We must also protect wildlife from poachers who illegally trap or kill animals.[9]

*A truckload of ducks and geese shot by poachers in one morning*
Courtesy of Saskatchewan Environment and Resource

7 Remember that saving our wilderness areas is the work and responsibility of all Canadians. We don't have much time left. We must act quickly if we are to save our wilderness heritage.

# II. Responding to the Article

## A. Journal Writing and Discussion

Spend the next 10 to 15 minutes writing in your journal about anything that interests you about the article. For example, your writing might include questions about information contained in the selection, or you may want to write about points made in the article with which you agree or disagree. When you have finished, form a group with two or three other people and read your responses to each other.

## B. Finding the Main Ideas

Remain in your groups. Discuss what you think are the main ideas that the author is trying to present. You may want to elect one person as "secretary" to write down the group's ideas. Be prepared to share your ideas with the rest of the class.

Read On Canada

# III. Comprehension Check

## A. Questions

**Part 1:** Work with members of your group to complete the following questions.

1. What is an ecosystem?
2. Why are ecosystems important?
3. What is happening to the prairie tallgrass?
4. How do we know if an animal is at risk of becoming extinct?
5. What are some of the ways we can protect our wilderness areas?

**Part 2:** Working with the members of your group, create five questions of your own about the article. These questions can be about specific ideas or information contained in the article, or about the meanings of particular words or phrases. When you have finished, exchange your questions with another group. Discuss the answers to the questions your group receives.

## B. True, False, and INP (Information Not Provided)

Work with a partner to complete the following exercise. Write "T" beside those sentences which are **true** and "F" beside those sentences which are **false**. Support your answer by using a sentence provided from the story. If the information in the sentence is not provided in the article, write **INP**.

1. _____ Plants and animals depend upon each other for their survival.

2. _____ New cars usually do not produce harmful chemicals.

3. _____ Birds are one type of species.

4. _____ Poachers do not kill park animals.

5. _____ Gold and nickel are minerals.

6. _____ Animals do not live in ecosystems.

7. _____ Pollution from factories pollutes our rivers.

8. _____ The World Wildlife Fund is an environmental group.

# IV. Word Power—Synonyms

Work with a partner to complete the following exercise. Circle the letter beside the answer that gives the same meaning as the word or expression in *italics*.

1. Canada is a country *made up of* different kinds of wilderness areas (paragraph 1).
   a. Canada has different kinds of wilderness areas.
   b. Canada's wilderness areas are all the same.
   c. Canada has very few wilderness areas.

2. In ecosystems, plants and animals live together with their surroundings and depend upon one another for their *survival* (paragraph 3).
   a. food
   b. lives
   c. death

3. Already in Canada, nine species of plants and animals have died out and become *extinct* over the past two hundred years (paragraph 4).
   a. increased in number
   b. survived
   c. disappeared

4. If we continue to destroy our wilderness areas at our current speed, all wilderness existing outside of parks or wilderness *reserves* will be gone within the next 30 years (paragraph 6).
   a. wilderness areas where wildlife doesn't live
   b. wilderness areas near cities
   c. wilderness areas protected from development

5. We must also protect wildlife from poachers who *illegally trap* or kill animals (paragraph 6).
   a. capture animals without breaking the law
   b. capture animals without anyone finding out
   c. capture animals even though it is against the law

# V. Active Interaction—An Endangered Forest

### Directions

Form a group with two other students and try to come up with a solution to the following problem.

You are members of a wilderness conservation group. A local logging company has asked for permission from the provincial government to cut down one of the oldest rain forests in Canada. Not only is this forest valuable because of its tremendous beauty, it is also one of the last places a rare species of bird can be found. Cut down the trees and the bird may not be able to survive. Added to this dilemma, the logging company must build a new road into the area so that trucks can carry out the logs. These roads will make it extremely easy for poachers to enter wilderness areas and illegally hunt and kill wild animals. How would you go about trying to convince the government not to allow the rain forest to be logged?

**Step 1:**  a.  Make a list on a large piece of chart paper of all the actions you could take (i.e., write letters, organize a protest, etc.). Write down your options under the heading "Possible Actions."

b.  After you have listed possible actions, think about the effectiveness of each action. Write down the effectiveness of each action you might take in an "Effectiveness" column.

c.  Next, decide which three actions your group thinks will be the most effective in convincing the government not to allow logging to take place. See the sample chart below.

## An Endangered Forest

| Possible Actions | Effectiveness |
| --- | --- |
| 1. | 1. |
| 2. | 2. |
| 3. | 3. |
| 4. | 4. |
| 5. | 5. |
| 6. | 6. |
| 7. | 7. |
| 8. | 8. |
| Most Effective Actions | Reason(s) For Choice |
| 1. | |
| 2. | |
| 3. | |

**Step 2:** Present your chart to the class and give reasons for your choices.

# VI. Further Topics for Discussion and Composition

1. How important is the preservation of wilderness areas in your native country or region of Canada? What steps has the government taken to protect wilderness from development?

2. Think about your home, classroom, or community. How would life be different if we did not develop our natural resources?

3. What types of outdoor activities do you like? How would they be affected by the loss of wilderness areas?

4. Should development companies be allowed to search for and extract resources located in provincial and federal parks? Why or why not?

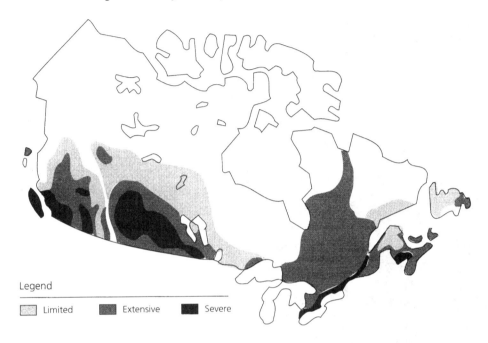

Legend: Limited | Extensive | Severe

Canadian wilderness areas are rapidly disappearing. What do the terms "limited," "extensive," and "severe" mean? What kinds of activities do you think are taking place in the shaded areas? So far, only about 3.4 percent of Canada is protected from forestry, mining, and other resource development. How do we strike a balance between development and protection of wilderness areas?

Courtesy of Wildlife Habitat Canada

5. Read the following article.

### CLAYQUOT SOUND PROTESTERS RECEIVE JAIL TERMS AND FINES

VANCOUVER — Stiff jail terms and fines were handed out today to 44 anti-logging protesters. B.C. Supreme Court Justice John Bouck sentenced the protesters to jail terms ranging from 45 to 60 days and fines ranging from $1500 to $3000. The sentences come a day after the protesters were found guilty of criminal contempt of court for defying a court injunction against blocking a MacMillan Bloedel logging road. The protesters were trying to prevent MacMillan Bloedel, a large forest company, from logging part of the old growth forest in Clayquot Sound on Vancouver Island. Supporters of the protesters branded the penalties as "harsh," but Bouck stated that, "Without the rule of law democracy will collapse. People will then be controlled by the rule of the individual. The strongest mob will rule over the weak. Anarchy will prevail."

Source: Vancouver Sun, October 15, 1993, p. A2.

The protesters described in this article were trying to stop a logging company from cutting down some of the last remaining stands of ancient west coast rain forest in Canada. The protesters believe that logging will not only destroy the trees, but will destroy entire ecosystems and the animals that live within them. They resorted to blocking the road after failing to convince the provincial government to halt logging in the area. Do you think that this type of "civil disobedience," or protest, was justified? Give reasons to support your opinion.

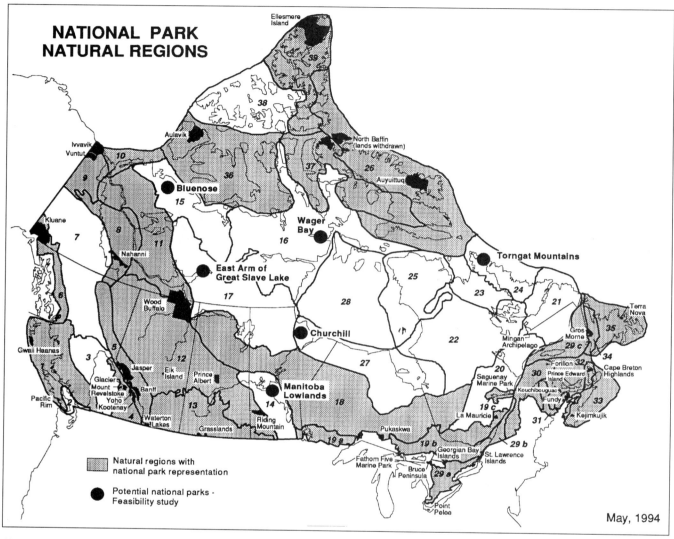

How many natural regions is Canada divided into? Which regions have you visited? Areas that may become national parks are marked on the map. What do you think a feasibility study is? What concerns and issues must be taken into account before an area is declared a national park?

Courtesy of Parks Canada

# VII. Learning Log

Open your journal and spend the next few minutes recording what you have learned and experienced from this particular unit. You may use your first language if this helps you to better express more complex ideas or insights.

# Just Another Load of Garbage?

## I. Pre-Reading Activities

### A. Before You Read

Before reading the article, complete the following activities with the rest of the class.

- When you throw something away, where does it go?
- What would you do if suddenly there was no more garbage collection service in your community?
- What does the term "recycling" mean to you?
- Make a list of some items that can be recycled.
- Share your list with the rest of the class.
- What do you think you will learn about in this article?

Go ahead and read the article. Try to guess the meaning of words that you do not know.

1. Canadians are in a garbage crisis. A crisis is a time of great difficulty or danger. Not only are we increasing the amount of garbage we produce each year, we are also running out of places to put it. In fact, as our mountains of trash continue to grow, the question of what we do with our garbage is becoming one of the biggest environmental problems facing us today.

2. Canadians are still among the biggest garbage producers in the world. On average, every Canadian creates about 2.2 kg of waste per person per day. That's over 30 million tonnes a year! In Sweden, on the other hand, each person is responsible for only about 0.8 kg per day.[1]

3. Garbage from homes makes up about 35–40 percent of the garbage created in Canada each year. The rest comes from institutional sources such as hospitals and schools, and from commercial sources such as restaurants and offices.[2] Most of the garbage we create goes directly into municipal landfills where it is dumped, incinerators where it is burned, or recycling depots where is it is sorted and reused. Unfortunately, there are problems associated with each of these disposal systems.

4. Canada has approximately 10 000 landfills located all across the country. They are usually located on agricultural land. As our need for landfill space increases, we lose more and more agricultural land for growing food. Some landfills also leak a chemical "tea" that pollutes our soil and water. They also give off toxic gases such as methane that contribute to the greenhouse effect and global warming.[3]

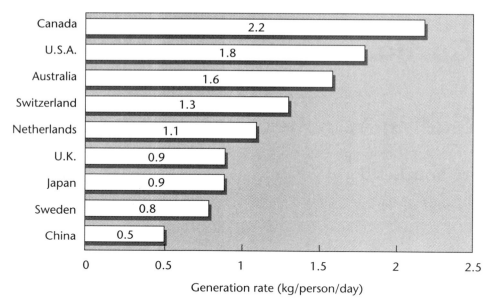

*Source:* British Columbia Ministry of the Environment: Program for Participation, September, 1990, p. 1.

5 Garbage placed in incinerators is simply burned. This solution seems easy, but it's not. Gases such as carbon dioxide that rise from the top of the smokestack also contribute to the greenhouse effect. Poisonous chemicals such as dioxins and heavy metals (like mercury) can also leave the smokestack and enter the atmosphere. These substances settle on the ground and pollute our water, soil, vegetation, and eventually our food.[4] While modern incinerators have significantly reduced or even eliminated the amount of pollutants released into the air during a burn, less modern facilities are still a major source of pollutants.

6 At recycling depots, materials such as glass, plastic, paper, and metal are separated out. Hazardous wastes such as household cleaners, paint, bug sprays, and weed killers are also removed. Unfortunately, because many people mix hazardous wastes with their regular garbage, many of these chemicals still reach the landfill.

7 Federal, provincial, and municipal governments, as well as numerous environmental organizations, are, however, working to reduce the amount of garbage we have to get rid of. For example, all levels of government have set a goal of reducing the amount of waste we produce by 50 percent from 1988 levels by the year 2000.[5]

8 Programs to cope with waste are generally based on the 3Rs—reduce, reuse, and recycle. Reducing the amount of waste we produce in the first place is the most important step. In many instances reducing our waste means only minor changes in our lifestyles. For instance, we can buy long-lasting items that can be repaired, or rent items rather than purchase them. Since disposable packaging and containers make up nearly 15 percent of our landfill space, we can avoid products with extra packaging.[6]

9 Reusing a product is a simple way of reducing our garbage. We can give away old furniture and clothing to non-profit organizations such as the Salvation Army. Buying items like soft drinks that come in refillable bottles also reduces our wastes.

10 Recycling is one of the most popular ways of reducing our garbage. One of the best ways for Canadians to recycle is by participating in local "blue box" programs. In these programs, householders are given a blue plastic box in which they can collect newspaper, glass, metals, and sometimes plastics. Municipal garbage collectors then pick up these materials and take them away for recycling.

*Just another load of garbage or valuable recyclables?*
Paul Sharples

*Recycling dramatically reduces the amount of waste we produce.*
Paul Sharples

11 In conclusion, the benefits of dealing more effectively with the amount of garbage we create are enormous. Landfills will not fill up as fast. Less money will be spent on getting rid of garbage. Also, less money and energy will be used searching for new resources to replace the ones we waste. Consequently, we can save millions of trees and preserve ecosystems. However, we can only be successful if each of us makes the personal decision to reduce the amount of garbage we produce. Only then can we "trash" our old habits and make Canada a less wasteful nation.

# II. Responding to the Article

## A. Journal Writing and Discussion

Spend the next 10 to 15 minutes writing in your journal about anything that interests you about the article. For example, your writing might include questions about information contained in the selection, or you may want to write about points made in the article with which you agree or disagree. When you have finished, form a group with two or three other people and read your responses to each other.

## B. Finding the Main Ideas

Remain in your groups. Discuss what you think are the main ideas the author is trying to present. You may want to elect one person as "secretary" to write down the group's ideas. Be prepared to share your ideas with the rest of the class.

# III. Comprehension Check

## A. Questions

**Part 1:** Work with members of your group to answer the following questions.

1. Why is the amount of garbage we create becoming a problem?
2. How can incinerators hurt the environment?
3. What are the 3Rs of recycling?
4. Give three examples of hazardous wastes in your own home.
5. Give five examples of recyclable materials.

**Part 2:** Working with the members of your group, create five questions about the article. These questions can be about specific ideas or information contained in the article, or about the meanings of particular words or phrases. When you have finished, exchange your questions with another group. Discuss the answers to the questions your group receives.

## B. True, False, and INP (Information Not Provided)

Work with a partner to complete the following exercise. Write "T" beside those sentences which are **true** and "F" beside those sentences which are **false**. Support your answer by using a sentence provided from the story. If the information in the sentence is not provided in the article, write **INP**.

1. _____ Canadians produce very little garbage.

2. _____ Methane is a toxic gas.

3. _____ We will probably solve our garbage problem by the year 2000.

4. _____ The United Kingdom is a bigger garbage producer than Canada.

5. _____ The Salvation Army is a non-profit organization.

6. _____ Aluminum is a heavy metal.

7. _____ Garbage from homes makes up 35–40 percent of our garbage.

8. _____ Hospital wastes are not dangerous to people.

## IV. Word Power—Cloze Encounters

Work with a partner to complete the following exercise. Use the context of the following sentences as well as information contained in the article to help you fill in the missing word. You can use each word only once. Capitalize words as necessary.

| commercial | wastes | institutional |
| crisis | trash | incinerator |
| landfills | recycling depot | disposal |
| toxic | reuse | global warming |
| collectors | hazardous | non-profit |

1. _____ chemicals can be harmful to our health.
2. Our garbage problem is becoming a _____.
3. Most of our garbage is simply dumped in _____.
4. Municipal _____ will pick up our recyclable materials.
5. Another word that means garbage is the word _____.
6. Garbage that comes from places such as schools and hospitals is known as _____ waste.
7. Recyclable materials are sent to a _____.

8. Heat from incinerators can contribute to _____.

9. We can send old clothes and furniture to _____ organizations like the Salvation Army.

10. If a chemical is _____ , it means it is dangerous.

# V. Active Interaction—How Do You Stack Up?

Here's an opportunity for you to stop and consider just what your contribution is—to both the problem and the solution.

**Directions**

Find a partner. Turn to the "How Do You Stack Up Checklist" on the next page. Take turns asking and answering the questions on the checklist. Circle the number that indicates your partner's response to each question and then add up the numbers to find out your partner's grand total. When you have finished turn to page 18 to find out how you stack up. Be prepared to discuss your results with other members of the class.

## How Do You Stack Up?

DO YOU...

|   |   | Never | Sometimes | Often |
|---|---|---|---|---|
| 1. | consider whether you really need something before you buy it? | 3 | 2 | 1 |
| 2. | think about what will happen to a product or package when you no longer need it? | 3 | 2 | 1 |
| 3. | try to reuse things you already have instead of disposing of them and buying new things? | 3 | 2 | 1 |
| 4. | consider what pollution and wastes were created in the manufacture of the things you buy? | 3 | 2 | 1 |
| 5. | take advantage of the opportunities in your area to recycle? | 3 | 2 | 1 |
| 6. | shop at second-hand stores or garage sales? | 3 | 2 | 1 |
| 7. | use dishcloths or sponges instead of disposable paper products which can never be recycled? | 3 | 2 | 1 |
| 8. | avoid items such as disposable diapers, razors or lighters when longer-lasting alternatives are available? | 3 | 2 | 1 |
| 9. | avoid eating in carry-out places that wrap your food in lots of paper and plastic, or ask that less wrapping be used for your order? | 3 | 2 | 1 |
| 10. | compost kitchen waste and other decomposable organic matter? | 3 | 2 | 1 |
| 11. | spend the money to repair an item even though you could buy a new one for nearly the same price? | 3 | 2 | 1 |
| 12. | talk to store managers about stocking bulk products or avoiding packaging? | 3 | 2 | 1 |
| 13. | complain to manufacturers about "built-in obsolescence"? | 3 | 2 | 1 |
| 14. | write to government officials expressing your concerns about the need to produce less wasteful products? | 3 | 2 | 1 |
| 15. | read consumer information articles to find out about the quality and durability of products you buy? | 3 | 2 | 1 |

Grand Total _____

*Source:* "How Do You Stack Up" reprinted with permission of B.C. Ministry of Environment, Lands and Parks from *Resources and Wastes Environmental Education Guide Teacher's Guide.*

## How Do You Stack Up?—Scores

IF YOUR SCORE WAS:

### 40 or more

Like most Canadians you are probably contributing your full share of waste to our rapidly filling landfills, including tons of usable, recoverable materials which are buried each day!

### What you can do!!

Be aware of the amount of garbage you have each day. Note how heavy it is. What could be reused, re-cycled, or avoided?

Next time you go to the store, check to see if any of the products you normally buy in non-recyclable containers are also available in returnable, refillable, or recyclable containers.

Call your nearest recycling depot for information on how, where, and when to recycle.

### between 21 and 39

You are doing some reducing, reusing, and/or recycling. These patterns need to be practised consistently by the majority of the population if we are going to reduce the increasing amounts of wastes.

### What you can do!!

Do some comparison shopping. Consider various types of packaging and the alternatives which are available. Does it cost more or less to buy reusable or recyclable packages?

Take your own grocery bags and plastic sacks back to the store and reuse them.

Call the nearest recycling depot about some items in your house you would like to recycle.

### 20 or less

You've obviously done some serious thinking about the need for resource recovery and conservation. It shows!

### What you can do!!

Think about the things you do to conserve. Which are you the most proud of? Encourage one other person to consider conservation.

Get involved in solid waste planning in your community.

Keep up the good work!

**LESS IS BETTER**
when it comes to garbage and energy consumption

# VI. Further Topics for Discussion and Composition

1. Discuss ways you can help reduce, reuse, and recycle wastes in your home.

2. You are the owner of a second-hand store and you have some wonderful "pre-owned" colour televisions. Write an advertisement for your store that will make people feel they should come in and make a purchase.

3. Look under "second-hand dealers" in the yellow pages. Note some of the store names. Rate them as "excellent," "average," or "boring." Give reasons for your choices.

4. Your city's garbage problem is getting worse and worse. Your landfill sites are full and there is no room to build new ones. The mayor has asked you, the head of the Waste Management Department, to find new uses for items that people have thrown away. For example, the mayor has suggested that you could use old toilet seats as picture frames, or old magazines as wallpaper. Create your list working with a partner or the whole class.

5. Product packaging has many purposes, including convenience, communicating information about the product, and sanitation. Think of five products that you have recently puchased. These products can come from different types of stores including fast food restaurants, grocery stores, gas stations, or clothing boutiques.

    a. Describe the packaging of each item.

    b. How could the package be reduced, replaced, or eliminated?

    c. Is the package reusable or recyclable? Explain.

    d. Do you think the packaging influenced your decision to buy the product? Explain.

    e. Think of a way you could improve the packaging of this product.

6. Design a "green kitchen," that is, a kitchen that reduces the amount of waste produced and makes it easy to recycle the wastes that are created. When planning your kitchen, consider the following:

    a. How can you reduce the amount of potential waste entering your home in the first place?

    b. How will you prepare food to minimize waste?

    c. How will you store food?

    d. One of the major problems with recycling household wastes is that they are often mixed together. How would you solve this problem?

    e. Will you need to create any new devices to make recycling easier? If yes, make sure you describe them in detail.

Read On Canada

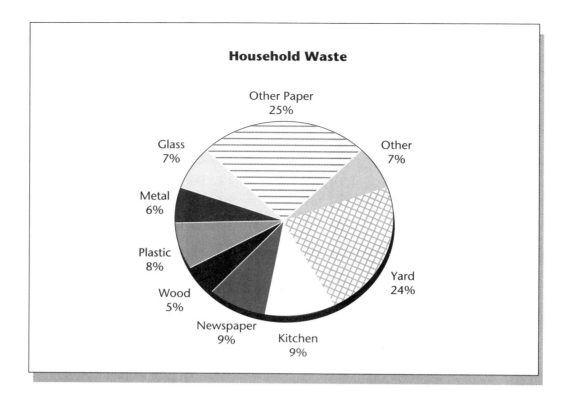

Source: *No Time To Waste,* Greater Vancouver Regional District Elementary Education Program p.18.

7. Ask your teacher to arrange a tour of a recycling operation in your area. If a tour isn't possible, you might be able to arrange for a guest speaker from an organization such as the Sierra Club to come to class to discuss all the various phases of the recycling process, and especially how it relates to your community.

# VII. Learning Log

Go back to your journal and spend the next few minutes recording what you have learned and experienced from this particular unit. You may use your first language if this helps you to better express more complex ideas or insights.

*Sun, Sea, Wind, and Sky*

# I-3 Saving the World by Cycling

Selling coconuts in Bukit Tinggi, West Sumatra, Indonesia
Paul Sharples

Taxi, anyone? Cholon, Vietnam
Paul Sharples

Family on the move in Ho Chi Minh City, Vietnam
Paul Sharples

Painter, Bukit Tinggi, West Sumatra, Indonesia
Paul Sharples

Read On Canada

# I. Pre-Reading Activities

## A. Before You Read

Before reading the article, complete the following activities with the rest of the class.

- Do you own a bicycle?
- What form of transportation do you use to get to school or work?
- How popular is cycling in your native country or region of Canada?
- What kinds of activities do people use bicycles for in your native country or region of Canada?
- What do you think you will learn about in this article?

Go ahead and read the article. Try to guess the meaning of words that you do not know.

1. Today, many of us are working hard to improve the quality of our lives. We exercise more often, eat healthier foods, and are committed to improving our natural environment. However, Canadians continue to overlook one of the major threats to human health and to the planet—cars.

2. Each year, worldwide, about 500 000 men, women, and children are killed in car accidents, and another 15 million are injured.[1] In addition, car exhaust emissions, the smoke, fumes, and chemicals discharged from a car's tail pipe, pollute our air and water, and are a major cause of lung and heart disease.[2] As well, roads and highways often destroy farmland and forests, and disturb the lives of animals.[3] Knowing these facts, more and more Canadians have decided to rediscover the bicycle.

3. Except for walking, bicycling is the main form of transportation in many parts of the world. In China, for example, bicycles outnumber cars 250 to 1. This figure equals approximately 300 million bicycles.[4] The Netherlands has more than 20 000 km of heavily used bike paths, and almost half of all trips in that country are taken on bicycles.[5] In Canada, we use our bikes mainly for recreation. However, in countries such as India and Indonesia, bikes serve many purposes. They are used to carry food, to make deliveries, and as ambulances. In Zaire they are even used by game wardens to chase down poachers.[6]

4. In fact, bicycles have many benefits over cars. The first is in the amount of energy they use. For 300 calories (an average breakfast) a person can travel about five kilometres. A car, on the other hand, needs the equivalent of about 18 000 calories to travel the same distance.[7] Bicycles do not cause any air pollution. Cars, meanwhile, produce millions of tonnes of ground-level ozone or smog. Smog contributes to acid rain and global warming. In addition, smog makes it difficult to breathe and can cause death among children and elderly people who suffer from asthma and bronchitis.[8] Smog also kills trees, contaminates the water, and damages wetlands. Ironically, cars pollute the most on short trips when the engine is cold and burns gasoline less efficiently. Since most people live less than 12 km from where they work, bikes could easily be used on such trips.[9] Bikes also take up a lot less space. Currently, about one-third of the area of most cities is used as parking lots and roads.[10]

5 There are also many other costs to owning a car besides to our health and environment. Each year throughout North America, billions of dollars are spent on building and fixing roads, public parking, and policing traffic. The productivity of many companies goes down because workers are spending time stuck in traffic jams. In Los Angeles, for example, by the year 2010 motorists will be spending more than half their waking hours in traffic jams.[11] In fact, as highways become more congested, bicycles are becoming faster than cars in getting through crowded downtown streets.[12] Police on bicycles are now even catching car thieves who get stuck in traffic![13]

6 Despite the many advantages of bicycling, many Canadians are still reluctant to give up their cars. In fact, only 2 percent of Canadian commuters use bicycles.[14] Many people feel that Canada's busy city streets are still too dangerous for bicyclists. Increasingly, city planners and politicians in many Canadian cities are working together with bicycling organizations to provide more marked bike paths and develop "bicycle-friendly" routes leading to downtown.[15] Employers are beginning to provide secure bike lockers as well as changing rooms and showers. In Montreal, it is now possible even to take your bicycles on the city's transit system.

7 Getting people out of their cars and onto their bicycles is more than just making it easier for bicyclists to move around, however. We must work on changing people's attitudes. Canadians need to understand that every time they choose to use a bike instead of a car they are helping to improve not only the quality of their lives but also the life of the planet. Knowing that means everyone can breathe a little easier.

# II. Responding to the Article

## A. Journal Writing and Discussion

Spend the next 10 to 15 minutes writing in your journal about anything that interests you about the article. For example, your writing might include questions about information contained in the selection, or you may want to write about points made in the article with which you agree or disagree. When you have finished, form a group with two or three other people and read your responses to each other.

## B. Finding the Main Ideas

Remain in your groups. Discuss what you think are the main ideas the author is trying to present. You may want to elect one person as "secretary" to write down the group's ideas. Be prepared to share your ideas with the rest of the class.

# III. Comprehension Check

## A. Questions

**Part 1:** Work with members of your group to answer the following questions.

1. How many people are killed each year in car accidents?
2. How does driving cars hurt the environment?
3. Name three other uses for bicycles besides recreation.
4. How can riding a bicycle make you healthier?
5. Is smog good for the environment? Why or why not?

**Part 2:** Working with the members of your group, create five questions of your own about the article. These questions can be about specific ideas or information contained in the article, or about the meanings of particular words or phrases. When you have finished, exchange your questions with another group. Discuss the answers to the questions your group receives.

## B. True, False, and INP (Information Not Provided)

Work with a partner to complete the following exercise. Write "T" beside those sentences which are **true** and "F" beside those sentences which are **false**. Support your answer by using a sentence provided from the story. If the information in the sentence is not provided in the article, write **INP**.

1. _____ There are millions of bicycles in Canada.

2. _____ Game wardens in Zaire use bicycles to catch poachers.

3. _____ Bicycles cause air pollution.

4. _____ About half of the people in the United States own bicycles.

5. _____ Canada makes some of the best bicycles in the world.

6. _____ Cars pollute the most on long trips, not short ones.

7. _____ Asthma is a type of heart disease.

8. _____ The police like to use bicycles.

# IV. Word Power—Antonyms

Work with a partner to complete the following exercise. From the list on the left, choose a word with the *opposite* meaning from the list on the right.

1. reluctant
2. disturbs
3. committed
4. healthy
5. contaminated
6. natural
7. rediscover
8. secure
9. congested
10. worldwide
11. dangerous
12. benefits

a. _____ apathetic
b. _____ affected
c. _____ conceal
d. _____ clean
e. _____ safe
f. _____ open
g. _____ eager
h. _____ disadvantages
i. _____ vulnerable
j. _____ local

# V. Active Interaction—The Transportation Committee

**Directions**

You are a member of your city's transportation committee. The provincial government has just given you a $10 000 000 grant to help improve the city's public transportation system. Your committee has received a number of submissions from various transportation organizations suggesting ways to achieve this. It is up to you and the other members of your committee to decide which organization's ideas you will adopt. Read the following submissions. Rank these ideas in order of importance. Rank what you think is the best suggestion as number 1 and the least useful suggestion as number 5. After you have made your own personal selection, get together with two or three other committee members and verbally compare your answers. Explain to the other members the reasons for your choices. Your group must come to an agreement on its choices. Be prepared to share your group's decisions with other groups.

a. The Society for the Upgrading of Bus Service suggests that the money be used to buy 20 city transit buses. This purchase would result in fewer cars on the road clogging city streets and highways, and less pollution.

b. The local Automobile Association suggests that the money be spent to widen the city's roads and to upgrade the city's bridges in order to make commuting to work by car less time-consuming. They also suggest that car-pool lanes be built to encourage people to car pool.

c. The Society for Alternative Transportation suggests that the money be spent on building bike routes throughout the entire metropolitan area. In addition, they suggest that the city begin a major public relations campaign to encourage drivers to "share the road" with bicyclists.

d. The Society for Intermodal Transportation (SIT) suggests that the money be spent on encouraging people to use more than one mode of transportation to reach their destinations. For example, they suggest that two extra rail cars be purchased for the city's rapid transit line. These cars would be for the exclusive use of commuters with bicycles. They also suggest that each public transit bus be equipped with bicycle carriers.

e. The Electric Car Society suggests the money be spent on the research and development of a low-cost electric car. They argue that with electric cars, air and noise pollution would be reduced.

## Transportation Committee Decision Chart

| Organization | Your Choice | Your Group's Choice |
|---|---|---|
| 1. Society for Upgrading Bus Service | Final ranking ____ <br><br> Reason(s) this group should/should not receive the money. | Final ranking ____ <br><br> Reason(s) this group should/should not receive the money. |
| 2. Automobile Association | Final ranking ____ <br><br> Reason(s) this group should/should not receive the money. | Final ranking ____ <br><br> Reason(s) this group should/should not receive the money. |

3. Society for Alternative Transportation

Final ranking ____

Reason(s) this group should/should not receive the money.

_____
_____
_____
_____
_____
_____
_____

Final ranking ____

Reason(s) this group should/should not receive the money.

_____
_____
_____
_____
_____
_____
_____

4. Society for Intermodal Transportation

Final ranking ____

Reason(s) this group should/should not receive the money.

_____
_____
_____
_____
_____
_____
_____

Final ranking ____

Reason(s) this group should/should not receive the money.

_____
_____
_____
_____
_____
_____
_____

5. Electric Car Society Transportation

Final ranking ____

Reason(s) this group should/should not receive the money.

_____
_____
_____
_____
_____
_____
_____

Final ranking ____

Reason(s) this group should/should not receive the money.

_____
_____
_____
_____
_____
_____
_____

# VI. Further Topics for Discussion and Composition

1. Discuss ways in which your city, town, or school can encourage people to use bicycles.
2. Write about an old bicycle, car, or some other form of transportation you have used in the past.
3. How important is the use of bicycles in your region of Canada or in your native country? Give examples.
4. What types of jobs could be effectively carried out on bicycles?
5. Discuss the advantages and disadvantages of riding a bicycle in a big city.

# VII. Learning Log

Go back to your journal and spend the next few minutes recording what you have learned and experienced from this particular unit. You may use your first language if this helps you to better express more complex ideas or insights.

## Word List: Crossword puzzle

| | | |
|---|---|---|
| CALORIES | LANDFILLS | SURVIVAL |
| COLLECTORS | OZONE | TALLGRASS |
| CONGESTED | POACHERS | TOXIC |
| CRISIS | REDUCE | TRASH |
| ECOSYSTEMS | RELUCTANT | VALUABLE |
| EMISSIONS | SPECIES | WASTES |
| INSPIRATION | | |

# Crossword Puzzle

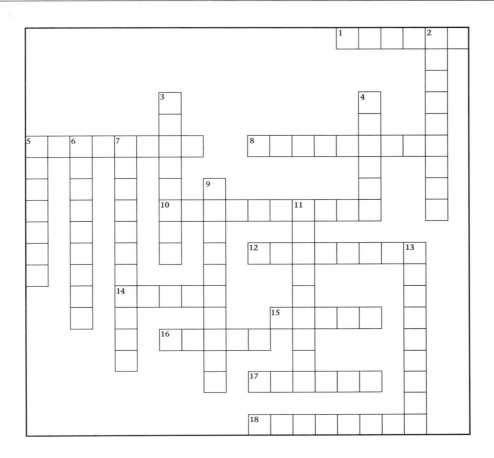

**Across**

1. _____, reuse, and recycle are the 3Rs of waste management.
5. In ecosystems, plants and animals depend on each other for their _____.
8. Most of the garbage we generate gets dumped into municipal _____.
10. Wetlands, forests, and even a small pond are examples of _____.
12. We sometimes damage wilderness areas when we dig for _____ minerals.
14. _____ chemicals can be extremely hazardous to our health.
15. Another word for garbage is the word _____.
16. Cars produce millions of tons of _____.
17. Canadians produce about 2.2 kilograms of _____ per person per day.
18. Riding a bicycle can help burn off a lot of _____.

**Down**

2. City highways are often _____ with cars.
3. People who illegally hunt animals are called _____.
4. Canadians are in the midst of a garbage _____.
5. Many of Canada's plants and animal _____ are now endangered.
6. Many Canadians are _____ to ride their bicycles to work.
7. Canada's wilderness areas have been an _____ to artists.
9. Municipal _____ will pick up our recyclable materials.
11. Much of Canada's prairie _____ has been turned into agricultural land.
13. Car _____ pollute the air.

## Chapter II

# TOWARD A HEALTHIER CANADA

# Dr. Peter: AIDS Educator

## I. Pre-Reading Activities

### A. Before You Read

Before reading the article, complete the following activities with the rest of the class.

*Dr. Peter*
David Gray

- What is AIDS?
- How do you become infected with it?
- Is AIDS a serious problem in your native country or region of Canada?
- How can we stop the spread of AIDS?
- What do you think you will learn about in this article?

Go ahead and read the article. Try to guess the meaning of unfamiliar words.

1 Acquired Immune Deficiency Syndrome, or AIDS, has become one of the deadliest epidemics of the century. An epidemic occurs when an infectious disease like AIDS spreads quickly from one person to another. The first confirmed cases of AIDS were reported in Canada in the late 1970s. Since then, approximately 8700 Canadians have caught the disease, and close to 6000 have died.[1] Some health experts estimate that by the year 2000 more than 110 million people worldwide could catch the disease.[2]

## All Known AIDS Cases in Canada—October 1993

| Age/Sex Group | Alive | Known Deaths | Total Cases |
|---|---|---|---|
| Adults | | | |
| Males | 2656 | 5450 | 8106 |
| Females | 153 | 294 | 447 |
| Subtotal | 2809 | 5744 | 8553 |
| Pediatric* | | | |
| Males | 17 | 29 | 46 |
| Females | 13 | 28 | 41 |
| Subtotal | 30 | 57 | 87 |
| Total | 2839 | 5801 | 8640 |

*less than 15 years of age.
Source: Health and Welfare Canada, Laboratory Centre for Disease Control

2 At present, there is no cure for AIDS. Treatments for the disease, which include radiation and chemotherapy (drugs), have had only mixed results. No one is even sure what causes the disease. Most doctors believe that the human immunodeficiency virus (HIV) causes AIDS. However, some doctors now believe that something else may be the source of AIDS.[3]

## Source of AIDS Infection in Canada (All Ages)

| Sources of Infection | Percentage of All Known Cases of AIDS in Canada |
|---|---|
| *Males* | |
| Homosexual/Bisexual activity | 81.5% |
| Perinatal* | 0.3% |
| Injection drug use (IDU)** | 2.0% |
| Homosexual/Bisexual activity and IDU | 3.8% |
| Blood recipient | 1.3% |
| Blood products | 2.1% |

| | |
|---|---|
| Heterosexual activity | 5.1% |
| No identified risk | 3.9% |
| *Females* | |
| Heterosexual activity | 57.0% |
| Perinatal* | 7.0% |
| Occupational exposure (one case) | 0.2% |
| Injection drug use** | 10.0% |
| Blood recipient | 13.9% |
| Blood products | 2.5% |
| No identified risk | 9.4% |

*Perinatal: These individuals were infected through transmission from their mothers either during pregnancy or birth, or through breast-feeding.
**Injection drug users were infected by sharing contaminated needles.
*Source:* Division of HIV/AIDS Epidemiology, BCDE, Laboratory Centre for Disease Control, Health Canada, October 1993

3 One of the most important weapons in the battle against AIDS is education. One of Canada's most powerful AIDS educators was a young Vancouver doctor named Peter Jepson-Young, or simply Dr. Peter. Dr. Peter was born on June 8, 1957, in New Westminster, British Columbia. After receiving an undergraduate degree in cell biology and working briefly as a bank teller, he was accepted at the University of British Columbia's medical school. He graduated as a doctor in 1985. On September 28, 1986, Dr. Peter was rushed to Saint Paul's Hospital in downtown Vancouver suffering from severe pneumonia. The next day his doctor told him he had AIDS. Despite the terrible news, Dr. Peter was determined to survive the disease. He continued to practise medicine, and maintained a full and active life.

4 Four years later, a colleague of Dr. Peter's came up with the idea of doing a video diary about AIDS. Dr. Jay Wortman, a Vancouver physician, had read about a similar series in the United States involving a television journalist in San Francisco. He approached Dr. Peter with the idea. Dr. Peter saw this as a wonderful opportunity to educate people about AIDS and agreed to his colleague's proposal. David Paperny of CBC Television agreed to produce the series which began in the summer of 1990. A three-minute segment was shown every Wednesday on the CBC Evening News in Vancouver. In each instalment, Dr. Peter would talk about how AIDS was affecting him physically and emotionally. He spoke in a calm, matter-of-fact way about how an AIDS-related viral infection was causing him to go blind despite all medical efforts to save his sight. When he eventually lost his sight completely, he described the challenges of being blind, and how blindness wasn't simply blackness but rather "like being in a very thick fog you know isn't going to clear."[4]

5 Dr. Peter also described his fight against an AIDS-related cancer called Kaposi's sarcoma. His medical knowledge allowed him to describe clearly how the cancer developed, and how it was quickly spreading throughout his body. He showed how the cancer had caused his right hand to become purplish and swollen, making it difficult for him to play the piano. In addition, he talked about how the drug and radiation therapy made him feel tired, feverish, and nauseated.

6 Even though the cancer spread to his lungs and throat and made it difficult for him to breathe, Dr. Peter continued to speak publicly about the disease both in Canada and abroad. In fact, he became so familiar that many people he had never met began to think of him as a friend and would stop him in the street to give him thanks and encouragement.

7 Dr. Peter did not simply talk about the disease itself. He also spoke about the difficulties of growing up gay in a society in which many people do not accept homosexuals as normal. He wanted people to understand that no one deserved the disease because of his or her lifestyle, and how a victim of AIDS could just as easily be a brother, a sister, or a best friend. He discussed how hard it was to tell his own parents he was gay, and how his friends and family supported him in his fight against the disease. In addition, he described the difficulties parents have in discussing the disease with their children. He also introduced us to his friend Harvey, a Canadian guide dog for the blind. Harvey was really "training him," he said, as they began to walk down the street together as if on a new adventure.[5]

8 Dr. Peter made over 100 diaries during a two-and-a-half year period. Over that time, he was able to educate thousands of people, many of whom had never met or known anyone with AIDS. His diaries became so popular that they have now been shown around the world and in 1994 were nominated for an Academy Award under the title, *The Broadcast Tapes of Dr. Peter*.

9 Dr. Peter died on November 15, 1992, at the age of 35. He is remembered for more than just his public battle with AIDS. Shortly before his death, he announced the establishment of the Dr. Peter AIDS Foundation. The purpose of the foundation is to provide financial support to AIDS patients so that they can use their energy to fight the disease and not have to worry about providing for their basic needs.

10 Dr. Peter has made a remarkable contribution in the fight against AIDS. Through his courage, determination, and suffering, he has helped put a name and a face on a terrible disease. He has made it easier for people with AIDS to speak out about their illness and their needs as individuals. Most of all, he has helped people to look beyond their fear of AIDS and work toward helping and supporting its victims. As Dr. Peter said himself, "If I have managed to reach out and educate people, to touch them and perhaps change their viewpoint about people with AIDS and gay people...then I think that will be my greatest contribution."[6]

# II. Responding to the Article

## A. Journal Writing and Discussion

Spend the next 10 to 15 minutes writing in your journal about anything that interests you about the article. For example, your writing might include questions about information contained in the selection, or you may want to write about points made in the article with which you agree or disagree. When you have finished, form a group with two or three other people and read your responses to each other.

## B. Finding the Main Ideas

Remain in your groups. Discuss what you think are the main ideas that the author is trying to present. You may wish to elect one person as "secretary" to write down the group's ideas. Be prepared to share your ideas with the rest of the class.

# III. Comprehension Check

## A. Questions

**Part 1:** Work with members of your group to answer the following questions.

1. Why did Dr. Peter make the video diaries?
2. How did the public react to the series?
3. What is the Dr. Peter Foundation?
4. What effect do you think the diaries will have on people's attitudes toward AIDS and gay people?
5. What do people in your native country think about AIDS?

**Part 2:** Working with the members of your group, create five questions of your own about the article. These questions can be about specific ideas or information contained in the article, or about the meanings of particular words or phrases. When you have finished, exchange your questions with another group. Discuss the answers to the questions your group receives.

## B. True, False, and INP (Information Not Provided)

Work with a partner to complete the following exercise. Write "T" beside those sentences which are **true** and "F" beside those sentences which are **false**. Support your answer by using a sentence provided from the story. If the information in the sentence is not provided in the article, write **INP**.

1. _____ There is no cure for AIDS.

2. _____ HIV causes AIDS.

3. _____ Dr. Peter was not a physician.

4. _____ Dr. Peter was 35 years old when he died.

5. _____ Kaposi's sarcoma is a type of cancer.

6. _____ Most people have never met anyone with AIDS.

7. _____ The Dr. Peter AIDS Foundation provides financial support to AIDS patients.

8. _____ AIDS didn't exist before 1970.

9. _____ The diary series began in the summer of 1991.

10. _____ We can protect ourselves from getting AIDS.

## IV. Word Power—Word Forms

In the sentences below, choose the correct form of the word.

| Noun | Verb | Adjective | Adverb |
| --- | --- | --- | --- |
| opportunity | | opportunistic/ opportune | |
| determination | determine | determined | |
| proposal/ proposition | propose | | |
| contribution | contribute | | |
| medicine | medicate | medicinal | medically |
| graduate/ graduation | graduate | graduated | gradually |
| confirmation | confirm | confirmed | |
| emotion | emote | emotional | emotionally |

1. Through his _____, Dr. Peter has helped to put a name and a face to AIDS.

2. Dr. Peter _____ as a medical doctor in 1985.

3. Dr. Peter said that he was glad to have had the _____ to educate people about AIDS.

4. The first _____ cases of AIDS appeared in Canada in the late 1970s.

5. Many people who knew Dr. Peter only through the video diaries reacted very _____ upon hearing the news of his death.

# V. Active Interaction—Tough Decisions

This activity is adapted from the game "Tough Decisions" in *The Nice Book*, Volume 2, by John Pak, YMCA, Yokohama, Japan.

### Directions

1. Take out a piece of paper. Write "yes" on one side and "no" on the other.
2. Your teacher will be asking you some questions. You will have about ten to twenty seconds to think about each question and then you must hold up your paper with your answer—*yes* or *no*.
3. Be prepared to give reason(s) for your answers.

### Questions

1. Your child comes home and tells you that her teacher is gay. Do you ask to have your child placed in another class?
2. A colleague at work wants to tell you an anti-gay joke. Do you tell him not to?
3. You find out that your friend's wife has AIDS. She wants it kept secret. Do you tell your friend anyway?
4. You are the Minister of Health. You must decide whether to spend your government's limited health budget to fight AIDS, which has killed relatively few people, or spend it on fighting heart disease, which is the number one cause of death in Canada. Will you spend the money on AIDS research?
5. You have a close friend who is dying of AIDS. There is no treatment for his condition. He does not want to suffer any longer. He asks you to help him end his life. Do you help?
6. You are about to get married. Your fiancée has just discovered that she contracted the AIDS virus from receiving HIV-infected blood during an operation. Do you still get married?
7. You are a dentist. One of your long-time patients has just informed you that he is infected with the AIDS virus. You are afraid that if other patients find out they will stop seeing you. Do you ask your patient to go somewhere else for dental treatment?

8. You are a doctor. One of your patients has AIDS. You discover that a new experimental drug is being used in the United States but is not yet legal in Canada. Do you try and get the drug for your patient anyway?

9. You have just discovered that you have contracted the AIDS virus. Do you tell your parents?

10. Your daughter arrives home from school and tells you that one of her classmates has AIDS. Do you allow your child to go back to that class?

# VI. Further Topics for Discussion and Composition

1. Many people believe that if a gay person or an intravenous drug user gets AIDS, it is his or her own fault. Do you agree? Give reasons for your answer.

2. Some governments do not allow people with AIDS to enter their countries. What is your opinion of such a policy?

3. Do you think you have a greater chance of getting AIDS if you are poor? Why or why not?

4. Many other diaries have been written by people who become famous after their death. *The Diary of Anne Frank* is a well-known example. How is a video diary different from a written diary? In what ways is it more effective? In what ways is it less effective?

5. Look at the information in the AIDS Stats box below and the world map on the next page. Given this information, what do you think can be done to help prevent the spread of AIDS in Canada and around the world?

## AIDS Stats

1. The Laboratory Centre for Disease Control, Health Canada, estimates that approximately 35 000 HIV-infected persons have lived in Canada. This figure includes people living with AIDS, those who are HIV-positive, and those who may have died from the disease.

2. The World Health Organization (WHO) estimates that every 30 seconds someone in the world is infected with HIV, the virus that leads to AIDS. Ninety percent of those individuals live in the developing world.

3. The WHO also estimates that there are currently about 750 000 cases of AIDS worldwide.

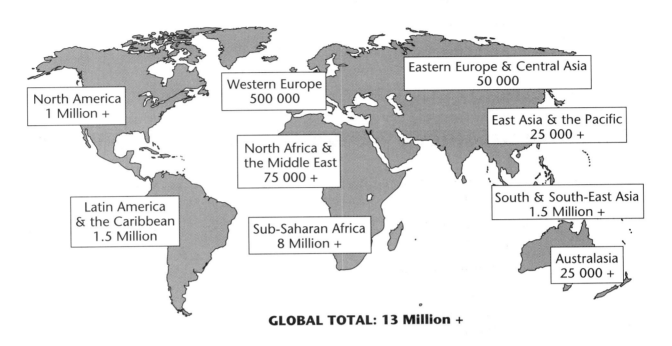

**Estimated Distribution of Cumulative HIV Infections in Adults, by Continent or Region: mid–1993**

Courtesy of the World Health Organization

## VII. Learning Log

Go back to your journal and spend the next few minutes recording what you have learned and experienced from this particular unit. You may use your first language if this helps you to better express more complex ideas or insights.

Read On Canada

# II-2 Of Shamans, Plants, and Healing

# I. Pre-Reading Activities

## A. Before You Read

Complete the following activities with the rest of the class before reading the article.

- Look at the title of the article.
- What does the word "shaman" mean?
- What do you think a shaman does?
- Are there shamans living in your native country or region of Canada?
- Do you think shamans can teach Western-trained doctors how to heal people?
- What do you think you will learn about in this article?

*Aymara folk healer in the mountains of Bolivia discusses the effectiveness of local remedies with Dr. R.W. Byard from the Department of Histopathology, Adelaide Children's Hospital, Adelaide, Australia.*
Courtesy of R.W. Byard

Go ahead and read the article. Try to guess the meanings of words that you do not know.

1. Plants have been used in traditional folk medicine for thousands of years. For many people in the developing world, plant-based therapies are the main method of treating illness. For example, the Qollahuaya in South America use over one thousand herbal cures.[1] However, very little research into the effectiveness of many of these treatments has been done in either Canada or the rest of the developed world.

2 For most of this century, in fact, many Western-trained doctors and researchers have thought of traditional folk medicine as either witchcraft or black magic. In addition, the men and women who practise traditional healing have been ignored or considered "quacks" by their modern counterparts.[2] Recently, however, researchers have discovered that folk healers and their medicines may have a much more valuable role to play in modern health care than anyone could have imagined.

3 It is true that immunization programs have been extremely effective against viral infections such as polio. However, one of the reasons for this increasing interest in traditional plant-based medicine is the failure of modern medicine to cure or adequately treat many of our common health problems. These include chronic pain, arthritis, migraines, and allergies, as well as many forms of cancer. Also, many modern drugs have side effects that range from drowsiness to kidney damage, and even to death. In addition, Western medicine does not work against viral infections such as various types of the flu, and, of course, AIDS.[3]

4 Many people in North America have also become more interested in "preventive" medicine, in other words, in stopping sickness before it starts. It has been suggested that traditional folk remedies such as garlic are effective in reducing the risks of getting some types of cancer and in helping to prevent heart disease.[4] Many doctors themselves have begun to use traditional medicine to give them added tools in treating their patients.[5]

*Preparing a prescription of Chinese herbs in Vancouver's Chinatown*
Paul Sharples

5 The fact that traditional plant-based remedies are providing new ways to treat disease is no surprise. Many commonly used medicines come from plants used in the ancient world. For example, many modern cold remedies contain ingredients from plants used in ancient China for over 5000 years.[6] In addition, folk healers in England used foxglove to treat heart problems nearly a thousand years ago. Today, digitalis, the drug made from foxglove, is used to treat heart failure as well as fever and asthma.[7] As well, Aboriginal peoples in North America have used the bark of the white willow tree to treat pain for hundreds of

years. Today, the chemical copy of salicin, the medicine found in the bark, is known to us as aspirin.[8] Also, reserpine, another traditional Aboriginal medicine, is used to treat high blood pressure. The rosy periwinkle, used by folk healers in Madagascar, is the source of vincritisine and vinblastine. These two chemicals successfully treat childhood leukemia.[9] Folk medicine of Central and South America has also been a rich source of modern medicine, including treatments for cancer and glaucoma.[10]

6 Many of these modern wonder drugs were brought to our attention by local witch doctors, shamans, and other traditional healers. For much of the developing world, these people are the main providers of health care. Consequently, many Western-trained health professionals are seeking their help in finding new ways to treat disease. In Madagascar, for example, scientists and local healers are working together to study just a few of the thousands of species of plants that grow on the island. Many of these plants have never been studied before and are not found anywhere else in the world.[11]

7 Similar research is taking place in many other countries including Canada, China, Japan, and Germany, as well as in Africa, and Central and South America. Much of the research is starting to show some promise. In Senegal, for example, scientists are using the local gueira plant to make a very effective cough syrup. In India, researchers are making anti-cancer drugs from local plants. Researchers in Paraguay are investigating over 3500 medicinal plants used in local folk medicine. Together with researchers from Japan and Germany, they hope to develop treatments for heart and liver disorders, rheumatism, arthritis, and diabetes, as well as many other diseases.[12] Research on the ginkgo tree is also showing some positive results. The ginkgo tree has been used in traditional medicine in China, Japan, and Korea for centuries to treat heart and lung problems. In Canada, drugs developed from a Chinese herbal root have stopped the spread of cancer cells in laboratory animals.[13] As well, it has been suggested that some traditional North American home remedies such as carrots and broccoli might be effective in reducing a person's risk of getting some forms of cancer.[14]

*Selling local herbal remedies on the street of New Delhi, India*
C.J. Clayton

8 Traditional plant-based medicine may yet hold the key to many of our modern illnesses. There are still many problems to overcome, however. Many researchers must continue to fight their own prejudice against traditional medicine. In addition, we must stop destroying the ancient rain forests. Approximately 25 percent of all medicines we use are made from rain forest plants. Unfortunately, the rain forest is being cut down at a rate of 1.5 acres per second; that's more than fifty million acres a year. This is particularly tragic because less than 1 percent of all rain forest plants have been scientifically studied.[15] As well, many developing countries have been abandoning traditional medicine in favour of expensive Western cures.

9 Unless governments promote the continued use of equally effective but less expensive folk remedies, important medical knowledge could be lost forever. Only if we work together with open minds will yesterday's folk myths become tomorrow's medical cures.

# II. Responding to the Article

## A. Journal Writing and Discussion

Spend the next 10 to 15 minutes writing in your journal about anything that interests you about the article. For example, your writing might include questions about information contained in the selection, or you may want to write about points made in the article with which you agree or disagree. When you have finished, form a group with two or three other people and read your responses to each other.

## B. Finding the Main Ideas

Remain in your groups. Discuss what you think are the main ideas that the author is trying to present. You may wish to elect one person as "secretary" to write down the group's ideas. Be prepared to share your ideas with the rest of the class.

# III. Comprehension Check

## A. Questions

Part 1: Work with members of your group to answer the following questions.

1. Why are Western scientists becoming more interested in traditional medicines?
2. What is preventive medicine?
3. What are the possible benefits of eating carrots and broccoli?
4. What is digitalis and how is it used?
5. What percentage of all medicines that we use come from rain forest plants?

**Part 2:** Working with the members of your group, create five questions about the article. These questions can be about specific ideas or information contained in the article, or about the meanings of particular words or phrases. When you have finished, exchange your questions with another group. Discuss the answers to the questions your group receives.

## B. True, False, and INP (Information Not Provided)

Work with a partner to complete the following exercise. Write "T" beside those sentences which are **true** and "F" beside those sentences which are **false**. Support your answer by using a sentence provided from the story. If the information in the sentence is not provided in the article write **INP**.

1. _____ Chemicals in some plants can help treat leukemia.

2. _____ Arthritis is caused by a virus.

3. _____ Western doctors do not use traditional medicine.

4. _____ Many of our modern-day cures come from plants.

5. _____ Chinese medicine has been practised for thousands of years.

6. _____ People are not interested in preventive medicine.

7. _____ Canadians prefer to use traditional medicine.

8. _____ Carrots and broccoli may help prevent some forms of cancer.

# IV. Word Power—Synonyms

Work with a partner to complete the following exercise. From the list on the left, choose a word with the *same* meaning from the list on the right.

1. myth          a. \_\_\_\_\_ conventional
2. effective     b. \_\_\_\_\_ unfortunate
3. prejudice     c. \_\_\_\_\_ potent

| | | | | |
|---|---|---|---|---|
| 4. | remedy | d. | _____ | illness |
| 5. | failure | e. | _____ | fable |
| 6. | tragic | f. | _____ | abundant |
| 7. | rich | g. | _____ | bias |
| 8. | abandon | h. | _____ | stop |
| 9. | risk | i. | _____ | leave |
| 10. | disorder | j. | _____ | cure |
| 11. | traditional | | | |
| 12. | prevent | | | |

# V. Active Interaction—New Wonder Drug Discovered

### Directions

You are part of a two-person news team that reports for a local newspaper. You have just heard that a new "miracle drug" has been discovered in the west coast rain forest. Your editor has ordered you and your partner to go to British Columbia, find out everything you can about this new drug, and write a story for your newspaper. Specifically, your boss wants to know the name of the new drug, where it comes from, what diseases it cures, how soon it will be available to Canadians, if there are any side effects, and how much the drug will cost to buy. The headline for your story will be: "New wonder drug discovered in west coast rain forest." Hurry, your deadline is fast approaching!

# VI. Further Topics for Discussion and Composition

1. How important is traditional medicine in your region of Canada or native country?
2. Describe an illness you once had that was successfully treated using traditional medicine.
3. Should a visit to a traditional folk healer in Canada be paid for by provincial medical insurance plans? Why or why not?

# VII. Learning Log

Go back to your journal and spend the next few minutes recording what you have learned and experienced from this particular unit. You may use your first language if this helps you to better express more complex ideas or insights.

Read On Canada

# II-3 The Sounds of Silence

## I. Pre-Reading Activities

### A. Before You Read

John McNeill

Before reading the article, complete the following activities with the rest of the class.

- Close your eyes and sit quietly for a few moments.
- Make a list of everything you hear.
- Imagine what life would be like if you couldn't hear these sounds. How would that make you feel?
- Write down as many words as you can to describe your feelings.
- What difficulties would you encounter in your everyday life if you could not hear?
- What do you think you will learn about in this article?

Go ahead and read the article. Try to guess the meaning of words that you do not know.

1 Imagine what it would be like not being able to hear your friend on the telephone. Or not being able to understand what your children are saying to you. Or imagine waking up one morning with a ringing in your ears that won't go away. One in ten Canadians suffers from a significant hearing loss and, for many, the culprit is exposure to excessive noise.

2 Excessive noise is harmful because it destroys the tiny hair-like cells in the inner ear that transmit sound to the auditory nerves. This type of damage is usually permanent. A sound can damage depending on how loud it is, as measured in decibels (dB), and how long we are exposed to it. For example, workers exposed to noise measuring 85 dB or above for more than eight hours could suffer a hearing loss.[1] Sounds at this level include industrial equipment, farm machinery, and sirens, as well as some home appliances. Over a quarter of a million workers are exposed to dangerous levels of noise across Canada every day.[2] Even professional athletes are not safe. The ping created when a baseball strikes an aluminum bat can produce a sound louder than 95 dB.[3] That's almost as loud as a table saw.

3 Of course the louder the noise, the less time it takes to cause damage to our hearing. For example, we can lose our hearing if exposed to a single loud sound of up to 140 dB or more.[4] Sounds in this range include firecrackers, gunshots, or explosions. Sounds of 75 dB or less usually have little effect on hearing.[5] This would include conversation, televisions, and vacuum cleaners.

4 One difficulty associated with noise-induced hearing loss is that it often occurs over a long period of time. Many people don't even realize they have a problem until they have suffered significant damage. Instead, they may deny they have a problem or accuse the people around them of mumbling. Getting people to speak louder or wearing a hearing aid cannot always solve the problem. Damage to the inner ear often means that a person cannot hear the message clearly because the sound is distorted.

5 One of the warning signs that tells us that we are being overexposed to noise is a ringing in our ears known as tinnitus. Rock musicians who are continuously exposed to high levels of intense noise often suffer from this condition. Tinnitus can be temporary, but if a person continues to be exposed to excessive noise, the condition can become permanent.

### SOUND LEVELS AND HUMAN RESPONSE

| COMMON SOUNDS | NOISE LEVEL (dB) | EFFECT |
|---|---|---|
| Jet engine (near) | 140 | |
| Shotgun firing / Jet takeoff (100-200 ft.) | 130 | Threshold of pain (about 125 dB) |
| Thunderclap (near) / Discotheque | 120 | Threshold of sensation |
| Power saw / Pneumatic drill / Rock music band | 110 | Regular exposure of more than 1 min. risks permanent hearing loss |
| Garbage truck | 100 | No more than 15 min. unprotected exposure recommended. |
| Average portable cassette player set above the halfway mark | ? | Are you setting your volume too high? Don't play auditory suicide. |
| Subway, motorcycle / Lawnmower | 90 | Very annoying |
| Electric razor, / Many industrial work places. | 85 | Level at which hearing damage (8 hrs.) begins. |
| Average city traffic noise | 80 | Annoying. Interferes with conversation |
| Vacuum cleaner / Hair dryer / Inside a car | 70 | Intrusive. Interferes with telephone conversation |
| Normal conversation | 60 | |
| Quiet office / Air conditioner | 50 | Comfortable |
| Whisper | 30 | Very quiet |
| Normal breathing | 10 | Just audible |

This dB table compares some common sounds and shows how they rank in potential harm to hearing. Recommended exposure times are based on current research.

*Source:* Canadian Hearing Society

6 How do you know if a sound is too loud? A good rule of thumb is that if you must raise your voice to be heard or cannot hear someone speaking to you from less than one metre away, you should probably wear some type of hearing protection such as earplugs. In addition, if a person sitting next to you can hear the music from your stereo headphones you should turn down the volume.

7 People are exposed to noise in a variety of settings. In the workplace, for example, construction and factory workers, miners, firefighters, and musicians work with extreme levels of noise. Fortunately, federal and provincial laws protect many of these workers. In Alberta, for example, a person cannot be exposed to noise levels of 95 dB for more than two hours and is not permitted to work in areas where the noise level reaches higher than 115 dB.[6]

8 For many people, the danger to our hearing occurs when we are not at work. For example, chain saws and snowblowers produce noise in the 95-118 dB range.[7] In addition, home appliances such as washing machines and dishwashers may by themselves produce safe levels of noise, but when added together they can become a problem.[8]

9 One of the biggest causes of hearing loss, however, is leisure noise. A hunter using a high-powered shotgun is exposed to a blast of up to 170 dB.[9] Rock concerts, snowmobiles, power boats, and even the symphony can expose us to sounds above 100 dB, or roughly the noise generated by a jet engine.[10] As well, car stereos and headphones connected to amplified sound put us at risk for hearing loss. One study of California school children discovered that 8 percent were already experiencing hearing loss.[11] In addition, audiologists at Scarborough General Hospital in Toronto report that increasing numbers of people in their twenties are suffering from hearing impairments.[12]

10 Young children are also exposed to potentially hazardous sounds. Many children's toys sold in Canada can cause a temporary or even permanent hearing loss. A child's cap gun can generate a sound level of 138 dB, louder than the sound of a jackhammer. Even a toy rattle can produce sounds up to 110 dB, equivalent to the noise produced by a chain saw.[13]

11 Besides hearing loss, exposure to excessive noise can lead to other problems, such as increased blood pressure and hypertension. Excessive noise can cause irritability, an inability to concentrate, and stress. Noise also affects learning and can lower children's reading scores.[14]

12 The great tragedy of noise-induced hearing loss is that it is mostly preventable. To protect our hearing we can simply avoid or limit our exposure to loud noise. We can wear hearing protection in noisy environments or when using noisy machinery. We can take breaks from listening to music or TV, and get regular hearing checks. Unless we take better care of our hearing, our ears may end up being attached to our heads only for looks.

# II. Responding to the Article

## A. Journal Writing and Discussion

Spend the next 10 to 15 minutes writing in your journal about anything that interests you about the article. For example, your writing might include questions about information contained in the selection, or you may want to write about points made in the article with which you agree or disagree. When you have finished, form a group with two or three other people and read your responses to each other.

## B. Finding the Main Ideas

Remain in your groups. Discuss what you think are the main ideas that the author is trying to present. You may want to elect one person as "secretary" to write down the group's ideas. Be prepared to share your ideas with the rest of the class.

# III. Comprehension Check

## A. Questions

**Part 1:** Work with members of your group to answer the following questions.

1. Why can leisure noise be dangerous to our hearing?
2. List some of the ways we can protect our hearing.
3. How do you know if a sound is too loud?
4. Why can't a hearing aid always solve a person's hearing problem?
5. What is tinnitus and how is it caused?

**Part 2:** Working with the members of your group, create five questions about the article. These questions can be about specific ideas or information contained in the article, or about the meanings of particular words or phrases. When you have finished, exchange your questions with another group. Discuss the answers to the questions your group receives.

## B. True, False, and INP (Information Not Provided)

Work with a partner to complete the following exercise. Write "T" beside those sentences which are **true** and "F" beside those sentences which are **false**. Support your answer by using a sentence provided from the story. If the information in the sentence is not provided in the article, write **INP**.

1. _____ Most Canadians suffer from a hearing loss.

2. _____ Excessive noise can damage our hearing.

3. _____ Leisure noise can be just as dangerous as industrial noise.

4. _____ Men have more hearing problems than women.

5. _____ The sounds made by some children's toys are not dangerous.

6. _____ The lead singer in a rock group usually has the worst hearing loss.

7. _____ Hearing loss can occur over a long period of time.

8. _____ A hearing aid allows a person to hear normally again.

# IV. Word Power—Synonyms

Work with a partner to complete the following exercise. Circle the letter beside the answer that gives the same meaning as the word or expression in *italics*.

1. One in ten Canadians *suffers* from a significant hearing loss (paragraph 1).
    a. enjoys
    b. endures
    c. ignores

2. Damage to the inner ear often means that a person cannot clearly hear the message because the sound is *distorted* (paragraph 4).
    a. too quiet.
    b. too loud.
    c. unclear.

3. A good *rule of thumb* is that if you must raise your voice to be heard or cannot hear some one speaking to you from less than one metre away, you should probably wear some type of hearing protection such as earplugs (paragraph 6).
    a. a generally held belief
    b. a myth
    c. a fact

4. One of the biggest causes of hearing loss, however, is *leisure noise* (paragraph 9).
    a. noise we are exposed to outside of work
    b. noise we are exposed to while on the job
    c. noise we are exposed to only during the daytime

5. The great tragedy of noise-induced hearing loss is that it is largely *preventable* (paragraph 12).
    a. unavoidable
    b. unnecessary
    c. unwelcome

# V. Active Interaction—Simulated Hearing Loss

It is difficult to imagine what life is like for a person with a noise-induced hearing loss. However, the following activities may give you some sense of what it is like trying to communicate without a sense of hearing.

1. Play team charades.

2. Plug your ears with cotton, choose a partner, and then discuss the difficulties a person with a severe hearing loss might have in everyday life.

# VI. Further Topics for Discussion and Composition

1. How could you convince a person who loves to listen to really loud music to change his or her behaviour?

Workers' Compensation Board of British Columbia

2. Look at the hearing protection poster above. At whom is the poster directed? Would this poster be effective in your school or workplace? Design your own hearing protection poster.

3. Make a "sound map" of your home, school, or workplace. Note common sources of noise in each area, and put a star beside sources of potentially excessive noise. Then write a brief summary of the sound level of your chosen environment.

4. Write to the Canadian Hearing Society at 271 Spadina Road, Toronto, Ontario, M5R 2V3, and request information on how we can prevent hearing loss.*

*Teacher, please note: The Canadian Hearing Society sells an excellent hearing loss simulation tape entitled *Getting Through*. This tape contains many excellent activities, including "The Unfair Spelling Test."

# VII. Learning Log

Go back to your journal and spend the next few minutes recording what you have learned and experienced from this particular unit. You may use your first language if this helps you to better express more complex ideas or insights.

## Word List: Crossword puzzle

| ABANDONING | DISTORTED | MUMBLING | SEGMENT |
| AMPLIFIED | EPIDEMIC | MYTH | TINNITUS |
| CHRONIC | FOLK | OPPORTUNITY | TRANSMIT |
| DECIBELS | FOUNDATION | PING | VIRAL |
| DETERMINED | HIV | PREJUDICE | |
| DIARY | LEISURE | QUACK | |

# Crossword Puzzle

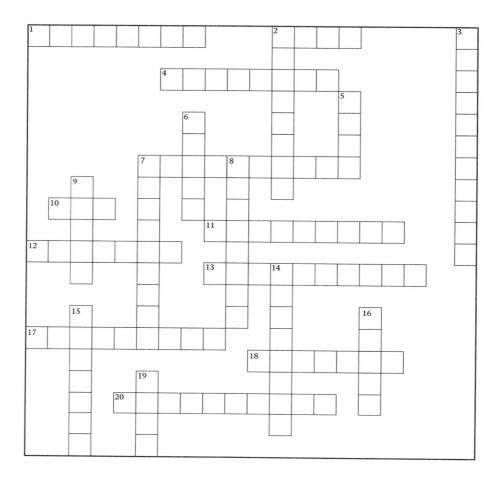

**Across**

1. A constant ringing sound in our ears is known as _____.
2. A very old folk _____ could provide answers for today's diseases.
4. Hair-like cells in the inner ear _____ sounds to the auditory nerves.
7. Many people are _____ the old ways of treating sickness.
10. Many doctors believe that _____ causes AIDS.
11. Sounds heard by a person with damage to the inner ear will be _____.
12. People have been turning to traditional medicine to treat _____ pain.
13. Dr. Peter was _____ to live a full life despite having AIDS.
17. Some western doctors must overcome their _____ to traditional medicine.
18. One of the biggest causes of hearing loss is _____ noise.
20. The Dr. Peter AIDS _____ was established in 1992.

**Down**

2. A person with a hearing loss often thinks people are _____.
3. Dr. Peter was glad to have had the _____ to tell people about AIDS.
5. The _____ from an aluminum bat is almost as loud as a table saw.
6. A person who pretends to be a doctor is called a _____.
7. People of all ages like to listen to _____ music.
8. We measure sound levels in terms of _____.
9. Dr. Peter's video _____ has been seen by thousands of Canadians.
14. AIDS is reaching _____ proportions in some parts of the world.
15. Each diary _____ in the Dr. Peter series was three minutes long.
16. The flu is a _____ infection.
19. _____ medicine has been practised for thousands of years.

# MISSING

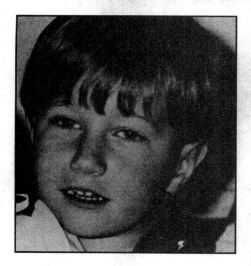
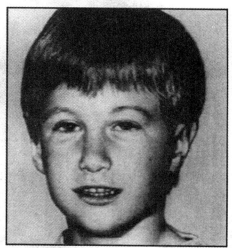

*Age Progression done by NCMEC*

**MICHAEL WAYNE DUNAHEE**
DOB May 12, 1986
Missing March 24, 1991 Non Family Abduction from
Victoria, BC Canada

At the time of his abduction Michael was 3 ft. tall and weighed 45 lb. He had sandy blonde hair and striking blue eyes. Michael was starting to show freckles when he disappeared.

## $200,000 REWARD FOR SAFE RETURN
Through Public Donation (In Trust)
**If you think you have seen Michael PLEASE CALL!!**

Victoria, BC Police Department 604-384-4111
IN CANADA Call Missing Children Society
1-800-661-6160
IN U.S. Call The National Centre for Missing and Exploited Children
1-800-843-5678

*Aged-progressed photos can assist police in locating missing children.*
Courtesy of the Michael Dunahee Search Centre

# TAKING ACTION AGAINST CRIME

*Taking Action Against Crime*

# High Tech Crime Fighting

## I. Pre-Reading Activities

### A. Before You Read

Before reading the article, complete the following activities with the rest of the class.

- What does the word "technology" mean?
- Tell the rest of the class about any recent technological developments that you are aware of.
- How do you think police in Canada use technology to help them solve crimes? List some examples.
- Do you think that there are some crimes the police in Canada would be unable to solve if they did not have technology to help them? Give some examples.
- What do you think you will learn about in this article?

Go ahead and read the article. Try to guess the meaning of words that you do not know.

1. Many crimes are difficult for police to solve. In one case, police may have only an old photograph to help them locate a long-lost child. In another case, they may have only a drop of blood or a single strand of thread to help link a suspect to a murder scene. In some instances, police may believe they have no clues at all to help them solve a case. However, recent technological developments are now allowing crime labs across the country to turn the most insignificant clues into important evidence.

2. Each year across North America, hundreds of children go missing. The best way for police to identify a missing child is, of course, to recognize a face. However, as the child grows older, this can be difficult. To overcome this problem, police hire artists to create drawings of what people will look like in the future. Artists are able to use a computer program designed by IBM Canada called the Computer Assisted Recovery System or CARES.[1] Many of these "aged-progressed" photos are placed on the sides of milk cartons or on posters in the hope that someone will recognize a missing child.[2] CARES is also used to help create a person's face using only his or her skull. It can also remove a disguise from a suspect's face and help create a composite drawing of a suspect from a witness's description.[3]

3. Computers can also help match fingerprints stored in police files with a suspect's. Previously, matching fingerprints was a time-consuming task that often ended in failure. In the United States, for example, the Federal Bureau of Investigation has more than 22 million fingerprint cards on file. Trying to find a fingerprint match from this mass of material was extremely difficult. The development of the Automatic Fingerprint Identification System (AFIS), however, changed all that. Police now use an optical scanner to read fingerprints taken from a crime scene. The information is then transferred to a computer and matched to fingerprints on file. This technology has led to a dramatic increase in the number of suspects identified.[4]

*Using a computer, Oak Bay Police Sergeant Ron Gaudet is able to obtain information in seconds about criminal activity across Canada and throughout the world.*

4 In addition to computers, police scientists use lasers to help catch criminals. Lasers help locate fingerprints on surfaces where they are normally difficult to find. For example, lasers can lift fingerprints from wood, plastic, rubber, and even human skin.[5]

5 One of the most powerful crime detection tools now available to police is genetic fingerprinting. Every cell in the human body contains genetic material called deoxyribonucleic acid, or DNA. With the exception of identical twins, every person's DNA is unique, just as everyone's fingerprints are unique.[6] Scientists can create a DNA fingerprint using body fluids such as blood, saliva, hair, or even a skin sample taken from a crime scene. Once the fingerprint is made, scientists can compare it to a suspect's or a victim's DNA. This technique helped convict Allen Légère of the murder of four women in New Brunswick in 1989.[7]

6 Canadian fish and wildlife officials use DNA fingerprinting in their fight to stop poaching. For example, wildlife officials in Alberta's Jasper National Park take blood samples of large elk and big-horned sheep. These samples are turned into DNA fingerprints and stored on file in a DNA library. A game warden can then determine if a particular animal has come from the park.[8]

7 Police also use technology to help locate illegal drugs. Drug dealers often try hiding drugs by mixing them with legal substances. Using a gas chromatograph mass spectrometer, for example, scientists can find a single grain of cocaine (one ten-billionth of a gram) in a kilogram of flour.[9]

8 Police also use powerful microscopes to determine the shape, the thickness, and even the colour of fibres too small to see. If these fibres are from a suspect's clothing, for example, police can often use them to place that individual at a crime scene.[10]

9 In addition, police labs use a technique called gunpowder fingerprinting to check if a suspect shot a particular gun. This technique involves studying the gunpowder residues left on the hand of someone who recently fired a gun. These residues create unique patterns that can be matched to the patterns left on the gun.[11]

10 As technology improves, police will be able to solve more and more cases they have been unable to previously. However, science cannot provide all the answers. Technology must still be combined with traditional, persistent police work if criminals are to be brought to justice.

# II. Responding to the Article

## A. Journal Writing and Discussion

Spend the next 10 to 15 minutes writing in your journal about anything that interests you about the article. For example, your writing might include questions about information contained in the selection, or you may want to write about points made in the article with which you agree or disagree. When you have finished, form a group with two or three other people and read your responses to each other.

## B. Finding the Main Ideas

Remain in your groups. Discuss what you think are the main ideas that the author is trying to present. You may want to elect one person as "secretary" to write down the group's ideas. Be prepared to share your ideas with the rest of the class.

# III. Comprehension Check

## A. Questions

**Part 1:** Work with members of your group to answer the following questions.

1. How can DNA fingerprinting be used to catch poachers?
2. Before the invention of optical scanners, why was it so difficult to match a suspect's fingerprints with those kept on file by the police?
3. How does CARES help police find missing children?
4. Why are fingerprints a good way of identifying a person?
5. How can microscopes help the police solve crimes?

**Part 2:** Working with the members of your group, create five questions about the article. These questions can be about specific ideas or information contained in the article, or about the meanings of particular words or phrases. When you have finished, exchange your questions with another group. Discuss the answers to the questions your group receives.

## B. True, False, and INP (Information Not Provided)

Work with a partner to complete the following exercise. Write "T" beside those sentences which are **true** and "F" beside those sentences which are **false**. Support your answer by using a sentence provided from the story. If the information in the sentence is not provided in the article, write **INP**.

1. _____ As missing children become older, they become more difficult to identify.

2. _____ Each person's fingerprints are not unique.

3. _____ CARES can help remove a suspect's disguise.

4. _____ Canadian police have more high-tech equipment than American police.

5. _____ If police find a fingerprint, they will always be able to solve a case.

6. _____ A genetic fingerprint can be made from a blood sample.

7. _____ Cocaine is not an illegal drug.

8. _____ Gunpowder residues can help police determine who fired a particular gun.

9. _____ Solving a crime depends on more than just high technology.

10. _____ Large elk and big-horned sheep are killed only for their meat.

# IV. Word Power—Cloze Encounters

Work with a partner to complete the following exercise. Write the correct word in each of the sentences below. You can use each word only once.

| | | | |
|---|---|---|---|
| unique | grain | lasers | residues |
| legal | scanner | DNA | mass |
| fingerprints | lift | suspect | insignificant |
| solve | scene | age-progressed | case |

1. Police use _____ photographs to help tell them what children will look like as they get older.

2. Even an _____ clue, like a strand of thread, can help police solve a crime.

3. The _____ was brought before a jury.

4. The gunpowder _____ from a recently fired gun can help police determine who fired the weapon.

5. There are a _____ of fingerprints on file with the FBI in the United States.

6. Except for identical twins, everyone's _____ are different.

7. It is not _____ to hunt animals without a licence.

8. Each person's fingerprints are _____ .

9. He is the main _____ in a murder investigation.

10. An optical _____ can help police match a suspect's fingerprints with those on police files.

11. Some crimes would be difficult to _____ without the use of high technology.

12. Until the invention of _____ , it was difficult to find fingerprints on surfaces such as wood.

# V. Active Interaction—Inventing a Techno Tool

### Directions

Work with two other students to complete the following exercise.

The chief of police is increasingly concerned about the rise in crime in your community. She has asked you, a famous inventor, and two of your colleagues to develop a new high-tech tool to help in the fight against crime. Working with other members of your team, design a new crime-fighting tool. Describe your invention and its potential uses to the rest of the class. Include a sketch and a suggested price for your new "techno tool."

# VI. Further Topics for Discussion and Composition

1. Most police forces have limited budgets. If they buy high-technology equipment, it usually means that they can hire fewer police officers. Do you think the police should continue to buy and use high-technology equipment even if it means that fewer police officers will be patrolling the streets? Explain your answer.

2. Some civil rights groups are concerned that a person's genetic information could be used for more than simply helping to catch criminals. They warn that genetic information could be used by employers to pick the best workers or by insurance companies to reject high-risk clients. They are also concerned that immigration officials could use genetic information to select the most favourable immigrants. Given these concerns, discuss how we might prevent the abuse of private genetic information.

3. How is crime the same or different in your native country compared to Canada?

# VII. Learning Log

Go back to your journal and spend the next few minutes recording what you have learned and experienced from this particular unit. You may use your first language if this helps you to better express more complex ideas or insights.

*Taking Action Against Crime*

# III-2 These Hackers Don't Play Golf

## I. Pre-Reading Activities

### A. Before You Read

Before reading the article, complete the following activities with the rest of the class.

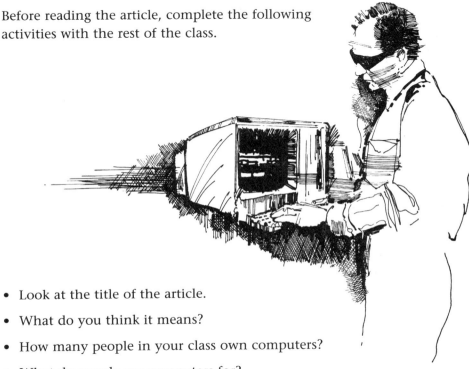

- Look at the title of the article.
- What do you think it means?
- How many people in your class own computers?
- What do people use computers for?
- How could people use computers to commit crimes?
- What do you think an "electronic cop" is?
- What do you think you will learn about in this article?

Go ahead and read the article. Try to guess the meaning of unfamiliar words. Try not to use your dictionary.

1 Every day Canadians are becoming more and more dependent on huge networks of computers to help us run our lives. Computers allow us to easily perform many routine activities from typing letters and withdrawing money to making telephone calls. They also help large financial institutions such as banks and credit card companies to operate quickly and accurately. However, as our dependence on computers grows, we become more and more vulnerable to attack from computer criminals known as hackers.

2 The name "hacker" refers to a whole group of people interested in how computer systems work. Hackers live all over the world. They are usually male and range in age from about 15 to 30. They also usually have an above average knowledge of computers and the systems that make them work.[1]

3 Some hackers like to break into a company's computer system without permission by using a computer modem. The modem connects the hacker's computer to other computers over simple telephone lines. Once inside the system, the hacker looks around and tries to find out how the computer system works. Most hackers will not deliberately damage or change a company's information files, or steal someone's financial records. After satisfying his or her curiosity, a hacker may simply depart or leave a message. Usually the message criticizes the company's poor security system and offers advice on how to improve it.[2]

4 Some hackers, however, are not so friendly. One group of hackers, known as "phone freaks," use their computers to erase voice-mail messages or to steal a firm's telephone access codes.[3] Once hackers have these codes, they use them to make computer phone calls all over the world. The long distance charges are then billed to the company.

5 Hackers use phone services to contact other hackers around the world on computer "chat lines" or electronic bulletin boards (BBS). Using code names such as Fibre Optik or Northern Phun, some chat line calls can involve up to 60 people at one time and last many hours.[4] For example, one Canadian hacker known as Entity broke into a computer system in Alberta so that he could use the system to contact a European chat line. By the time he and ten other hackers had finished talking, the phone bill had reached $20 000.[5]

6 Hackers also use these chat lines to learn more about computers or to exchange stolen telephone access codes. Mostly, however, they like to boast about the various computer systems they have broken into. This way, they earn respect and recognition from other hackers.[6]

7 It is also on these chat lines that destructive hackers, also known as cyberpunks or phreaks, learn about some of the more sinister aspects of hacking. For example, hackers can obtain credit card numbers stolen from credit card company computers. Hackers can also learn how to make explosives, change computer files, or spy on a company's electronic mail system.[7] For example, an American hacker named Fry Guy used a stolen credit card number to obtain $6000 in cash from Western Union from December 1988 to July 1989.[8] The problem has become so bad that telephone and credit card companies in North America are each losing over a billion dollars a year to hacker crime.[9]

8 Some of the most destructive hackers create computer viruses to cause trouble. Viruses are programs that enter a computer, usually hidden inside a company's regular software. Once inside a word processing program or a game, the virus looks for other programs to infect. Since companies often link computers on a network, a virus can spread throughout an entire system very quickly.

9 Some viruses are harmless. For example, a Bulgarian hacker named the Dark Avenger created a virus that made the computers in one California company play the song "Yankee Doodle" every eight days at five p.m. While the virus itself didn't cause any damage, the company had to close down for several days to get rid of it.[10]

10. Some viruses, however, can change or destroy important data, or cause entire computer systems to stop working. In 1988, for example, a Cornell University student named Robert Morris shut down the Internet computer network using a type of virus known as a worm. This Internet network is used by research institutes and universities throughout North America. After only four hours, 6000 computers across the United States stopped working. The cost of the damage was $90 million.[11]

11. According to the RCMP, less than 10 percent of hacker crime is reported to the police.[12] Companies are usually embarrassed about being broken into and are afraid their customers will lose confidence in them. A lot of hacker crime goes undetected because a hacker is often extremely skilful. Some hackers can break into a system, get the information they need, and then leave without anyone finding out.

12. "Outside" hackers, however, do not commit the majority of serious computer crimes. The greatest threat to computer security comes from hackers who work for the company.[13] These employees will usually damage a system or steal money, either because they are angry at the company or because they are having financial or marital problems.[14]

13. Sometimes hackers will even help police catch a particularly malicious hacker. For example, when a hacker named Wasp began to tamper with computers at Bell Communications Research in the U.S., another hacker, known as Control-C, helped company officials trace Wasp.[15]

14. Many large companies throughout the world are working hard to protect themselves from being "hacked." Bell Canada, for instance, has installed sophisticated security programs and has formed its own computer security team.[16] These "hacker trackers," or electronic cops, monitor the company's computer network looking for any unusual activity on the system. Some computer security firms suggest that employees sign an oath to keep all company information secret.[17] As well, the police are beginning to monitor hacker chat lines and shut down those involved in illegal activities.[18] Unfortunately, many firms cannot afford expensive security systems or simply do not take the hacker threat seriously.[19]

15. Despite improvements to computer security and the arrest of prominent hackers such as Wasp, hacker crime continues to grow. Companies must continue to work diligently to protect their computer systems and must not underestimate the skill and patience of the electronic underground. Only in this way can we successfully pull the plug on hackers.

# II. Responding to the Article

## A. Journal Writing and Discussion

Spend the next 10 to 15 minutes writing in your journal about anything that interests you about the article. For example, your writing might include questions about information contained in the selection, or you may want to write about points made in the article with which you agree or disagree. When you have finished, form a group with two or three other people and read your responses to each other.

## B. Finding the Main Ideas

Remain in your groups. Discuss what you think are the main ideas that the author is trying to present. You may want to elect one person as "secretary" to write down the group's ideas. Be prepared to share your ideas with the rest of the class.

# III. Comprehension Check

## A. Questions

**Part 1:** Work with members of your group to answer the following questions.

1. Describe one way hackers can learn about computer systems.
2. How can hackers make free long distance phone calls?
3. What is a computer virus and what can it do?
4. Why are companies now hiring "electronic" cops?
5. Why does most hacker crime go unreported?

**Part 2:** Working with the members of your group, create five questions about the article. These questions can be about specific ideas or information contained in the article, or about the meanings of particular words or phrases. When you have finished, exchange your questions with another group. Discuss the answers to the questions your group receives.

## B. True, False, and INP (Information Not Provided)

Work with a partner to complete the following exercise. Write "T" beside those sentences which are **true** and "F" beside those sentences which are **false**. Support your answer by using a sentence provided from the story. If the information in the sentence is not provided in the article, write **INP**.

1. _____ Some computer viruses are harmless.

2. _____ A BBS is an electronic chat line.

3. _____ Most computer hackers come from the United States.

4. _____ Most hackers do not intend to damage a computer system.

5. _____ Robert Morris helped police catch a hacker name Fry Guy.

6. _____ A worm is a type of computer virus.

7. _____ Most hackers get caught.

8. _____ Stealing telephone access codes is legal in Canada.

9. _____ Small companies often cannot afford expensive computer security systems.

10. _____ Control-C is the name of a Canadian security agent.

# IV. Word Power—Antonyms

Work with a partner to complete the following exercise. From the list on the left, choose a word with the *opposite* meaning from the list on the right.

1. malicious
2. shut down
3. secure
4. dependent
5. spread
6. erase
7. confidence
8. deliberate
9. curious
10. patient
11. prominent
12. diligent

a. \_\_\_\_\_ bored
b. \_\_\_\_\_ unknown
c. \_\_\_\_\_ kind-hearted
d. \_\_\_\_\_ accidental
e. \_\_\_\_\_ add
f. \_\_\_\_\_ uncertainty
g. \_\_\_\_\_ lazy
h. \_\_\_\_\_ impatient
i. \_\_\_\_\_ start up
j. \_\_\_\_\_ confine

# V. Active Interaction—Hacker Trapper Interview

### Directions

You are an employee of the Big Canadian Bank. You have just helped the police arrest the notorious hacker named the Keyboard Crusader. This dastardly criminal was trying to break into your bank's computer system, empty everyone's bank account, and transfer all the money to himself. However, you found a way to stop him. Now you are a hero and your local newspaper wants to interview you.

1. First read the newspaper reporter's questions and then write down your answer.
2. When you finish, find a partner. One person asks the questions while the other answers using his or her own answers. Then change roles.

Reporter: Good morning and thank you for your time.

Hacker Trapper: _____

Reporter: How long have you worked at the Big Canadian Bank?

Hacker Trapper: _____

Reporter: What is your job with the bank?

Hacker Trapper: _____

Reporter: How did you find out that someone was trying to break into your computer system?

Hacker Trapper: _____

Reporter: Very interesting. How were you able to stop the hacker from damaging your computer system?

Hacker Trapper: _____

Reporter: Remarkable. How were you able to lead police to where the hacker was living?

Hacker Trapper: _____

Reporter: That close? What was your reaction when you found out that the hacker had been arrested by the police?

Hacker Trapper: _____

Reporter: I can believe it. What was your boss's reaction when she found out that you had stopped the Keyboard Crusader from robbing the bank?

Hacker Trapper: _____

Reporter: What will you do in the future to help prevent hackers from breaking into your computer system?

Hacker Trapper: _____

# VI. Further Topics for Discussion and Composition

1. Some computer experts believe that hackers are a valuable part of the computer world. In what ways do you think a hacker might be able to help the computer industry?

2. Why do you think that most hackers are young men?

3. Do you think it is good that we are becoming so dependent on computers? What problems do you think might occur?

4. Some people are "computer resistant," that is, they do not want to learn to use computers. Why is this?

# VII. Learning Log

Go back to your journal and spend the next few minutes recording what you have learned and experienced from this particular unit. You may use your first language if this helps you to better express more complex ideas or insights.

Read On Canada

# Building Community Partnerships

## I. Pre-Reading Activities

### A. Before You Read

Before reading the article, complete the following activities with the rest of the class.

*News conference outlining the centre's anti-auto theft program*
Courtesy of Chinatown Police Community Services Centre

- Write down the word "police."
- Now write down all the words you associate with "police."
- What is the relationship between the police and the people in your native country.
- What do you think is the role of the police?

- How can police work with community members to help prevent crime?
- Look at the photo on the previous page.
- What do you think this place is?
- What do you think happens there?
- What do you think you will learn about in this article?

Go ahead and read the article. Try to guess the meanings of words that you do not know.

1  With the composition of our immigrant population changing, Canada is becoming a more racially and culturally diverse nation. For example, by the turn of the century, almost half of the population of Metro Toronto will be made up of visible minorities.[1] This change creates many new challenges for police forces and ethnic communities. In fact, the relationship between police and some ethnic communities can best be described as one of mutual distrust and misunderstanding.[2]

2  The reasons for this poor relationship are complex. Some members of ethnic groups believe that many police officers view community members through narrow cultural stereotypes. They believe that they are not treated equally by the police, and that the police are insensitive and do not deal effectively with their concerns. In addition, some immigrants come from countries where the police sometimes torture and kill people who resist the local government. Consequently, when they arrive in Canada, the police are the last people they will call upon for help.[3]

3  The police, for their part, are being asked to perform an already demanding and dangerous job within an increasingly complicated work environment. They receive little or no cross-cultural awareness training[4] and, in many instances, have had little positive contact with ethnic minorities. They also believe that their actions are often misunderstood. For example, they may be accused of harassment while simply answering a complaint from another citizen. In fact, some police officers feel that they are in a "no-win" situation and will be accused of racism no matter how they react.[5]

4  Both sides agree, however, that one of the ways to address feelings of mutual distrust is by developing cooperative and constructive relationships. One approach to fostering better police-ethnic relations is the development of community-based police stations.

5  One of these "storefront" stations has been established in the heart of Vancouver's Chinatown district. Established in April 1992, the Chinatown Police Community Services Centre is a project developed by the Chinese community, the provincial government, and the Vancouver Police Department. The aim of the centre is "to strengthen the communication and cooperation between the Chinese community and the Police department."[6] The centre attempts to achieve this goal by making police services more accessible to the community and by encouraging public input on those services.

6  The centre is operated by paid non-police staff and volunteers who provide services in Mandarin, Cantonese, Vietnamese, and English. The centre also operates with the assistance of the Police Oriental Liaison Unit. The police officers who are a part of this unit often speak both English and the languages of the community. It is their job to help initiate

and maintain contacts with businesses and social and cultural groups within the Oriental community. They patrol the Chinatown area on foot which not only makes them more accessible to community members but helps to increase the police profile in the area. It also allows the police to have better contact with the community and helps them develop new approaches in helping to prevent crime.

7 The centre provides services for groups or individuals. For example, the centre provides public education on crime prevention programs such as Block Watch, Block Parents, and Crime Stoppers. In addition, it provides information on police services as well as traffic and driving safety. The centre also writes a column in one of Chinatown's daily newspapers which provides information to the community on a variety of important issues involving the police.

8 The centre also offers a victim assistance program that includes counselling and referrals to legal and social services, as well as help in completing a criminal injury compensation application. The centre also provides services to witnesses of a crime. These include help in reporting a crime, translation services, and establishing contact with the police department. People reporting a crime do not have to identify themselves and can report to either a staff member or to one of the Oriental Liaison Unit officers.

9 Another important function of the centre is that it encourages members of the community to consider a career in policing. This role is particularly significant because racial minorities are poorly represented in police forces across Canada.[7]

10 While the centre has received positive feedback from both the police and community groups, it will take some time before it is widely accepted by the community as a whole. Barriers between police and the community still exist. However, the Chinatown Police Community Services Centre represents an important and innovative approach in helping to build community partnerships, in preventing racial and cultural misunderstandings, and, of course, in helping to prevent crime.

# II. Responding to the Article

## A. Journal Writing and Discussion

Spend the next 10 to 15 minutes writing in your journal about anything that interests you about the article. For example, your writing might include questions about information contained in the selection, or you may want to write about points made in the article with which you agree or disagree. When you have finished, form a group with two or three other people and read your responses to each other.

## B. Finding the Main Ideas

Remain in your groups. Discuss what you think are the main ideas that the author is trying to present. You may want to elect one person as "secretary" to write down the group's ideas. Be prepared to share your ideas with the rest of the class.

# III. Comprehension Check

## A. Questions

**Part 1:** Work with members of your group to answer the following questions.

1. What are some of the reasons given why some ethnic communities in Canada have a poor relationship with the police?

2. In paragraph 3, what does the expression a "no-win situation" mean?

3. Which crime prevention programs mentioned in the article have you participated in, if any?

4. Do you think that storefront police stations are an effective way to help prevent crime? Give reasons for your answer.

5. What are some other ways that the police and local communities can work together to help prevent crime?

**Part 2:** Working with the members of your group, create five questions about the article. These questions can be about specific ideas or information contained in the article, or about the meanings of particular words or phrases. When you have finished, exchange your questions with another group. Discuss the answers to the questions your group receives.

## B. True, False, and INP (Information Not Provided)

Work with a partner to complete the following exercise. Write "T" beside those sentences which are **true** and "F" beside those sentences which are **false**. Support your answer by using a sentence provided from the story. If the information in the sentence is not provided in the article, write **INP**.

1. _____ Some members of certain ethnic groups think many police officers view them through cultural stereotypes.

2. _____ The police in some countries sometimes torture people.

3. _____ Only police officers operate the Chinatown storefront station.

4. _____ The aim of the centre is to strengthen communication and cooperation between the Oriental community and the police.

5. _____ The centre does not offer translation services.

6. _____ Ethnic minorites are underrepresented on Canada's police forces.

7. _____ The centre has been operating for over twenty years.

8. _____ The centre provides a number of different crime prevention programs.

## IV. Word Power—Word Forms

In the sentences below, choose the correct form of the verb.

| Noun | Verb | Adjective | Adverb |
|---|---|---|---|
| referral/reference | refer | | |
| accessibility/access | access | accessible | |
| civilian | civilize | civil | |
| stereotype | stereotype | stereotypical | stereotypically |
| | foster | foster | |
| initial | initiate | initial | initially |
| perception | perceive | perceived | perceptively |
| construction | construct | constructive | constructively |

1. After forty-five years in the military, he was finally a _____ again.

2. The city's Police Ethnic Relations Committee developed some very _____ ideas for preventing crime in the community.

3. Storefront police stations make the police more _____ to the public.

4. The new police commissioner said she would _____ some new and innovative changes in the police force.

5. The police are often _____ as racist by some members of Canada's ethnic communities.

# V. Active Interaction—Police Ethnic Relations Committee Interview

**Directions**

You are a prominent member of your ethnic community who has been asked to attend a meeting of your local Police Ethnic Relations Committee. The committee is currently holding meetings to try to find ways that the police and members of your community can work together to better understand each other and to help prevent crime.

1. First read the committee's questions and write down your answers.
2. When you finish, find a partner. One person asks the questions while the other answers using his or her own answers. Then change roles.

Committee chairperson: Good afternoon. Thank you for coming.

Community member: _____

Committee chairperson: Could you tell us how long you have been living in the area?

Community member: _____

Committee chairperson: How safe do you feel when you walk alone in your neighbourhood at night and during the day?

Community member: _____

Committee chairperson: Hmm. In what areas of your neighbourhood do you feel unsafe?

Community member: _____

Committee chairperson: What are the some of the most common types of crimes being committed in your neighbourhood?

Community leader: _____

Committee chairperson: Oh, that's very unfortunate. What is the relationship between the local police and members of your ethnic community?

Community leader: _____

| | |
|---|---|
| Committee chairperson: | Would you please give us some examples? |
| Community leader: | _____ |
| Committee chairperson: | What are some important aspects of your ethnic community that you think the police should know about so that they can better understand the needs of the community? |
| Community leader: | _____ |
| Committee chairperson: | I see. What types of crime prevention programs would you like the police to start in your neighbourhood? |
| Community leader: | _____ |
| Committee chairperson: | That's very interesting. What other ideas do you have about improving safety in your neighbourhood? |
| Community leader: | _____ |
| Committee chairperson: | Those are some excellent ideas. Thank you for coming. It has been a pleasure meeting you. |

# VI. Further Topics for Discussion and Composition

1. You are the chief of police in your city. Currently no members of ethnic minorities are on the police force. The mayor has asked you to design an advertising campaign to encourage members of ethnic minorities to apply. Your campaign can include posters, pamphlets, and even television commercials.

2. Describe an encounter that you once had with the police either in your native country or in Canada. Give as much detail as possible about the incident. Was it a positive or negative experience? How did it affect your feelings about the police?

3. Find out what the requirements are for joining the police force in your area. What kind of person do you think would make the best police officer? Why?

4. Write out five questions that you have always wanted to ask a police officer (but maybe were afraid to ask).

5. How is the role of the police in Canada different from the role of the police in your first country? Give examples to support your statements.

6. Play the Great Canadian Crime Game on the following page.

Taking Action Against Crime

# The Great Canadian Crime Game

**Directions**

a. Form groups of three or four.

b. Read the following questions and write down your answer to each question. Place your answer in the "My Guess" column.

c. After you have made your own choices, compare your answers with those of the others in your group.

d. The group should now try to come to an agreement on what the best answer to the question is. You should mark your answer in the column called "Group's Guess."

e. Be prepared to share the reason(s) for your group's choices with the rest of the class.

f. Take your time going through the questions. Each one provides an excellent basis for discussion.

|  | My Guess | Group's Guess |
|---|---|---|
| 1. What has been the average annual increase in violent crimes committed in Canada since 1977? Give your answer as a percent. |  |  |
| 2. According to the 1993 Violence Against Women Survey, what percentage of violent incidents against women are reported to police? |  |  |
| 3. Common assault (a threatened assault or an actual assault that did not produce a serious physical injury) makes up what percentage of all violent crimes committed against Canadians? |  |  |
| 4. In which province are you most likely to be murdered? |  |  |
| 5. Am I at higher risk of being a victim of a homicide if I live in a large urban area or a small urban area? |  |  |
| 6. How is a person most likely to be murdered in Canada? |  |  |
| 7. Are men or women more likely to be murdered? |  |  |
| 8. What percentage of individuals accused of homicides are male? |  |  |
| 9. What percentage of all homicides are committed by persons known to the victim? |  |  |
| 10. By what percentage has the number of people charged with impaired driving decreased over the past ten years? |  |  |

|  | My Guess | Group's Guess |
|---|---|---|

11. What is the national rate of persons charged with impaired driving per 10 000 persons in Canada?

12. What percentage of robbery incidents involves a weapon?

13. Approximately how many motor vehicles are stolen in Canada each year?

14. What percentage of federal male inmates were under the influence of alcohol or other drugs when committing at least one of the crimes that led to their current sentences?

15. Is the risk of being robbed greater for males or females?

16. Are people over the age of 65 more or less likely to be victims of a violent crime?

17. Are you more likely to be the victim of a homicide if you are single or married?

18. What percentage of robberies are committed by females?

19. What percentage of persons convicted of robbery are sent to prison?

20. Are you more likely to be robbed if you are male or female?

21. Does a woman 65 years of age and over have a greater or lesser chance of having her purse snatched?

22. Is an arsonist (someone who deliberately lights fires to cause damage) more likely to set fire to a single home or to a commercial location?

23. Are you more likely to be a victim of arson in Canada or in the United States?

24. What percentage of victims of violent crime are teenagers (12–19 years)?

25. Is a person under 12 years of age more likely to be a victim of a violent incident in a residence or at school?

26. What is the most common type of theft under $1000 committed by female youths (aged 12–17)?

27. If you are a female youth (aged 12–17) and you are tried for minor assault, what are the chances that you will be found guilty?

*Taking Action Against Crime*

|  | My Guess | Group's Guess |
|---|---|---|
| 28. If you have your car stolen, what are the chances that it will be recovered? | | |
| 29. Over the past 20 years, by what percentage has the number of stolen vehicles risen in Canada? | | |
| 30. Are you more or less likely to have your car stolen if it cost over $10 000? | | |
| 31. Where are you more likely to have your car stolen, from the street or from a shopping centre parking lot? | | |
| 32. Are you more likely to have your car stolen between 9:00 p.m. and 6:00 a.m. or between 6:00 a.m. and 9:00 p.m.? | | |
| 33. What percentage of owners who have their vehicles stolen left their keys in the vehicle at the time of the theft? | | |
| 34. What are the chances that, if your vehicle is stolen, it will be damaged when you get it back? | | |
| 35. What percentage of motor vehicles are stolen for the purpose of joyriding (driving the car for fun, usually recklessly)? | | |

*Source:* Statistics Canada, *Report on Crime 1992* and *Juristat 1992–1994*.

# VII. Learning Log

Go back to your journal and spend the next few minutes recording what you have learned and experienced from this particular unit. You may use your first language if this helps you to better express more complex ideas or insights.

## Word List: Crossword puzzle

| | | | |
|---|---|---|---|
| ACCESSIBLE | DIVERSE | MALICIOUS | SOLVE |
| AIDS | DNA | MASS | STEREOTYPES |
| AIM | ERASE | MATCHING | SUSPECT |
| BARRIERS | FINGERPRINTS | MINORITIES | SYSTEM |
| BOAST | GRAIN | MODEM | UNIQUE |
| CODES | HACKER | PERCEIVE | VIRUS |
| CONSTRUCTIVE | INPUT | SCENE | |
| CRIME | LIFT | SOFTWARE | |

# Crossword Puzzle

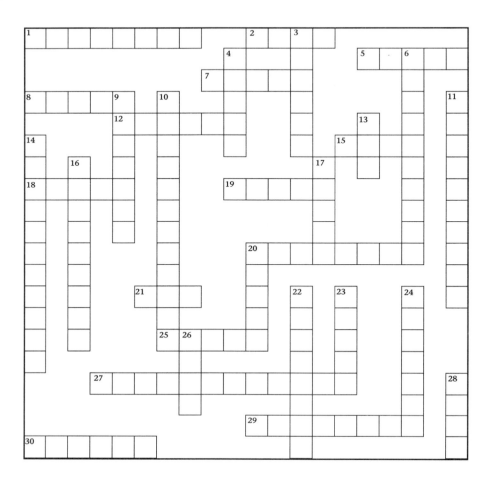

**Across**

1. Previously, _____ fingerprints was a very time-consuming task.
2. A chromatograph _____ spectrometer is used to detect drugs.
5. Hackers often _____ about the computer systems they break into.
7. Some hackers steal telephone access _____.
8. One type of computer _____ is known as a worm.
12. Each person's fingerprints are _____.
15. The centre helps or _____ victims.
18. Some viruses can _____ important information files.
19. Machines can detect a single _____ of cocaine in a kilogram of flour.
20. _____ is a small disk or tape that contains computer programs.
21. Scientists can create _____ fingerprints from body fluids such as blood.
25. Many crimes are extremely difficult to _____.
27. People have developed some _____ ideas for preventing crime.
29. Some ethnic groups _____ the police as being racist.
30. A _____ is a kind of computer criminal.

## Down

3. Hackers like to illegally break into a company's computer _____.
4. A _____ lets you use send and receive computer information on the phone.
6. Storefront police stations make the police more _____.
9. This person is the main _____ in the murder investigation.
10. Police now use an optical scanner to help match _____.
11. Ethnic _____ will soon make-up the majority of some city's populations.
13. _____ or goal.
14. Some Canadians view ethnic minorities through narrow cultural _____.
16. Some hackers are extremely _____.
17. To help solve crime, the police need _____ from the community.
20. A crime _____ can yield valuable information about a crime.
22. Canadians of colour still encounter racial _____.
23. Technological advances help us to fight _____.
24. Canada is made up of people from _____ cultural backgrounds.
26. Many company employees must take an _____ that they will not "hack".
28. Police are now able to _____ fingerprints from surfaces such as wood.

*Serving up smiles at a seniors' dinner*
Canada Wide Feature Services

# Chapter IV

# PROTECTING AND PROVIDING

# IV-1 Wronged and Rights

## I. Pre-Reading Activities

### A. Before You Read

Before reading the article, complete the following activities with the rest of the class.

- Imagine that one day at work you overhear your boss making jokes about your ethnic background.
- Imagine finding a note on your desk that says "Non-whites not welcome in Canada."
- Make a list of words that describe how you would feel.
- Share your list with the rest of the class.
- What does the word "harass" mean?
- What do you think the term "racial harassment" means?
- What do you think we can do to stop racial harassment from happening?
- What do you think you will learn about in this article?

Go ahead and read the article. Try to guess the meaning of words that are unfamiliar to you.

1 Most Canadians believe they live in a tolerant and generous society where people of all races, creeds, and colours are treated equally. Sadly, this belief does not reflect what is actually happening in Canada. Racism is alive and well, and has existed in this country ever since French explorer Jacques Cartier first made contact with Aboriginal peoples in the Gulf of St. Lawrence over 450 years ago.

2 One of the ways racism expresses itself is in racial harassment in the workplace. According to Canadian human rights legislation, racial harassment is a form of discrimination based on a person's race, colour, or national or ethnic origin.

3 Racial harassment can be subtle or overt and can begin even before a person is employed by a company. For example, investigations by the Canadian Civil Liberties Association and the Ontario Human Rights Commission found that some employment agencies would willingly refer only job applicants who were white when asked to do so by an employer.[1] When members of a visible minority are granted interviews, they are often denied jobs without satisfactory reasons.[2] In one instance, a black woman in Winnipeg was told that a job she had applied for had been filled even though she knew the employer was still interviewing.[3]

4 Once employed, members of visible minorities can encounter many different types of racial harassment. For example, a black employee who worked for a federal government department received a letter through the office's internal mail system containing numerous racial slurs. Added to this, when he complained to his managers they failed to take his concerns seriously.[4] In British Columbia, an Indo-Canadian man working for a major fast food restaurant was subjected to numerous racist comments and epithets by his senior managers.[5] In yet another incident, an Ontario government employee suffered continual anti-Chinese jokes and found anti-Chinese graffiti in his immediate work area, as well as racist posters that remained for several days in the building's elevators. When the employee complained to his supervisor, his complaints were ignored.[6]

5 In addition to racial slurs, jokes, letters, and graffiti, harassment can also take the form of an increase in workload and supervision, an unsatisfactory evaluation, or being overlooked for promotion for no valid reason.[7] Whatever form it takes, racial harassment can have a devastating impact on its victim. It can lead to stress, humiliation, depression, sleeplessness, and absenteeism. It can also create tension in the workplace that directly affects a company's production and causes able people to quit their jobs. As well, unless action is taken to stop racial harassment, it can create an air of acceptability for such behaviour and possibly lead to physical violence.[8]

6 Unfortunately, many minority workers are unaware of their rights under federal and provincial human rights law or they are simply afraid to complain for fear of reprisal. This is particularly true of minority women who often occupy low-paying, unskilled, dispensable jobs, and whose opportunities for other employment are limited.

7 It is possible, however, for workers to take immediate and effective action to stop racial harassment. Such action can include letting the harasser know that his or her actions are unwanted. This approach may be particularly effective if a person unintentionally commits racial harassment because of ignorance about the beliefs and values of another person's culture or race. An individual can also write a letter of complaint to an administrator, or file a grievance if he or she is a member of a union.

8 Victims of racial harassment can also file complaints with the federal or provincial human rights commission. Human rights commissions have the right to investigate and try to settle a dispute between an employee and an employer. If attempts at early settlement fail, the commission will then make a decision about the case. If an employer is found guilty, the commission can order such action to stop, issue a fine, or order an employer to pay compensation to the employee. Compensation can include letters of apology, the establishment of an anti-harassment policy by the employer, compensation for lost wages, and the return of the person's job. For example, the Ontario Human Rights Commission ordered the owner of a major electronics company to pay $293 000 as part of a settlement package to four senior managers who were fired for refusing to carry out a "whites-only" hiring policy.[9] In Manitoba, three Winnipeg Hydro employees were awarded $1500 each by the Manitoba Human Rights Commission because a supervisor had subjected them to racial slurs for eight years.[10]

9 Employers can be convicted of racial harassment even if they were completely unaware that one of their employees was racially harassing a fellow worker. Under Canadian

human rights law, preventing workplace harassment is the responsibility of the employer. Also, under federal human rights law, employers can be fined up to $50 000 if they threaten or try to intimidate an employee who has filed a complaint.

10 Whatever action a victim of racial harassment decides to take, it is important to gather as much information as possible about the incident.[11] It is up to the employees to prove that they have been a victim of racial harassment. If an individual is uncertain about what to do, he or she can contact local support groups, such as the Canadian Anti-Racism Education and Research Society, or the appropriate provincial or federal human rights commission, as well as the local Legal Aid office. It is also important for a victim to have the support of friends and co-workers. Racial harassment can often make a person feel afraid, vulnerable, and isolated.

11 Every Canadian has the right to employment or to receive a service without harassment in any form. While many employers are working to eliminate racial harassment in the workplace by offering programs on multiculturalism and employment equity, and by developing and enforcing strict anti-harassment policies, there is still a long way to go. As long as one group of people holds on to the belief that it is somehow superior to another group, racial harassment will continue, and Canada will never realize its potential as a nation.

# II. Responding to the Article

## A. Journal Writing and Discussion

Spend the next 10 to 15 minutes writing in your journal about anything that interests you about the article. For example, your writing might include questions about information contained in the selection, or you may want to write about points made in the article with which you agree or disagree. When you have finished, form a group with two or three other people and read your responses to each other.

## B. Finding the Main Ideas

Remain in your groups. Discuss what you think are the main ideas that the author is trying to present. You may want to elect one person as "secretary" to write down the group's ideas. Be prepared to share your ideas with the rest of the class.

# III. Comprehension Check

## A. Questions

Work with members of your group to answer the following questions.

1. What are some of the forms that racial harassment can take?
2. Why can racial harassment affect a company's production?
3. What types of compensation for racial harassment can an employer be told to give an employee?
4. Why do you think many minority women are employed in low-paying dispensable jobs?
5. What effects can racial harassment have on an individual?

**Part 2:** Working with the members of your group, create five questions of your own about the article. These questions can be about specific ideas or information contained in the article, or about the meanings of particular words or phrases. When you have finished, exchange your questions with another group. Discuss the answers to the questions your group receives.

## B. True, False, and INP (Information Not Provided)

Work with a partner to complete the following exercise. Write "T" beside those sentences which are **true** and "F" beside those sentences which are **false**. Support your answer by using a sentence provided from the story. If the information in the sentence is not provided in the article, write **INP**.

1. _____ Many employers are trying to eliminate racism in their workplaces.

2. _____ There are severe legal penalties for racial harassment.

3. _____ Racial harassment never hurts anyone.

4. _____ Some ethnic groups are more racially harassed than others.

5. _____ Racism only developed in Canada over the past ten years.

6. _____ It is possible to take effective action against racism in the workplace.

7. _____ Racial harassment can sometimes be unintentional.

8. _____ Racial harassment can create tension in the workplace.

# IV. Word Power—Synonyms

Work with a partner to complete the following exercise. From the list on the left, choose a word with the *same* meaning as the word in the list on the right.

1. convict
2. compensate
3. subtle
4. isolated
5. promote
6. dispensable
7. tolerant
8. creed
9. overt
10. reprisal
11. harass
12. grievance

a. _____ retaliation
b. _____ separated
c. _____ encourage
d. _____ find guilty
e. _____ belief
f. _____ complaint
g. _____ bother
h. _____ obvious
i. _____ unprejudiced
j. _____ insinuated

# V. Active Interaction—What would you do if...?

**Directions**

1. Form a group with three or four other people.
2. Read the following cases and discuss what action you would take in each situation.
3. Write down your options in the "Possible Actions" column.
4. Think about the consequences of each action. Write down the consequences of each action you take in the "Consequences" column.
5. Next, decide which action(s) your group would choose to take and why.
6. Be prepared to share your choices with the rest of the class.

**Scenario 1**

You have started a new job and look forward to working and gaining some experience. However, on the first day of work, one employee calls you names, tells jokes about your background, and openly makes fun of the way you look, speak, and dress. This staff member makes your life at work extremely difficult.

| Possible Actions | Consequences |
|---|---|
| 1. | 1. |
| 2 | 2. |
| 3. | 3. |
| 4. | 4. |
| 5. | 5. |

Action(s) taken and why:

---

### Scenario 2

You or a friend works in a restaurant where there are customers who always tell jokes about your background and openly make fun of the way you look, speak, and dress. You want them to stop bothering or harassing you.

| Possible Actions | Consequences |
|---|---|
| 1. | 1. |
| 2 | 2. |
| 3. | 3. |
| 4. | 4. |
| 5. | 5. |

Action(s) taken and why:

---

### Scenario 3

Your younger brother, who walks with a limp, comes home from school and tells you that some kids were teasing him about the way he looks and speaks. He is very upset over this.

| Possible Actions | Consequences |
|---|---|
| 1. | 1. |
| 2 | 2. |
| 3. | 3. |
| 4. | 4. |
| 5. | 5. |

Action(s) taken and why:

Scenario 4

Your friend's younger sister comes home from school and reports that kids were teasing her about her ethnic background and were calling her racist names. She is very upset over this.

| **Possible Actions** | **Consequences** |
| --- | --- |
| 1. | 1. |
| 2 | 2. |
| 3. | 3. |
| 4. | 4. |
| 5. | 5. |

Action(s) taken and why:

*Source:* Acknowledgement to Mr. Hayne Wai of the Canadian Human Rights Commission for permission to use this activity.

# VI. Further Topics for Discussion and Composition

1. People differ on what they believe is the cause of racial harassment. What do you think are the reasons someone tells racist jokes or makes racist comments?

2. Imagine that you have just found a racist poster taped to the top of your desk. Write a letter to your boss describing the poster, how you feel about it, and what you would like your boss to do about the incident.

# VII. Learning Log

Go back to your journal and spend the next few minutes recording what you have learned and experienced from this particular unit. You may use your first language if this helps you to better express more complex ideas or insights.

Read On Canada

# IV-2 In Service of Others

Marko Shark

Canada Wide Feature Services

## I. Pre-Reading Activities

### A. Before You Read

Before reading the article, complete the following activities with the rest of the class.

- Look at the pictures above.
- What is happening in these pictures?
- Who do you think these people are?
- What does the word "volunteer" mean?
- Have you ever been a volunteer?
- Share your experiences with the rest of the class.
- What types of work do volunteers do?
- What would happen if no one ever wanted to volunteer?
- What do you think you will learn about in this article?

Go ahead and read the article. Try to guess the meaning of new words from their context in the sentence.

1 Canada is a nation of volunteers. Each year, more than 5 million Canadians freely donate some of their time, skills, and energy to help make Canada a more caring and

compassionate nation. Their efforts range from raising money to finance new hospital facilities to visiting the sick or elderly to helping feed starving children in developing countries. Whatever form it takes, volunteering is seeing a need and doing something about it.

2 There is no such person as a typical or average volunteer. Canadian volunteers come from every age group. They may be rich or poor, working or unemployed, have a university degree or never attended high school. They are drawn together, however, by a desire to improve and enrich the lives of the people they meet.

3 Canadians volunteer for a wide variety of reasons. According to a Statistics Canada report entitled "Giving Freely," the volunteers surveyed said that helping others, supporting a cause, and doing something they like to do were the most important reasons why they volunteered.[1] Other reasons people volunteer include a desire to meet other people, learn new skills, and gain experience to improve job opportunities. People will also volunteer in response to a crisis, such as the famine in Ethiopia.

4 Working either alone or as part of an organization, volunteers provide a wide variety of services. For example, Canadians who volunteer with religious organizations are often involved in fund raising, education, and providing food and shelter for people who are sick, poor, and elderly. Canadians also coach teams, organize festivals and fairs, and act as interpreters for those who speak English as an additional language. They are also involved in self-help groups such as Alcoholics Anonymous and the Friends of Schizophrenics. Many Canadians also work with social agencies to provide counselling and support for single parents, victims of sexual assault, street youth, and drug addicts. They join environmental and animal protection organizations such as the Western Canada Wilderness Committee and the World Wildlife Fund. They also participate in crime prevention programs such as Block Watch and Crime Stoppers. As well, Canadians join organizations such as OXFAM-Canada and Canada World Youth that provide education and development programs to people living both in Canada and abroad.

5 While volunteers are needed by hundreds of organizations, volunteering does not have to make a large demand on a person's time. An individual can volunteer whenever and wherever he or she likes. For example, volunteering may mean driving an elderly person to the store once a month to pick up groceries, joining a walk for hunger, or simply donating old clothing to a refugee settlement program.

6 While volunteering has many personal benefits, it can at times be very difficult. A person working with a terminally ill patient may have to come to terms with his or her own fear of death. Volunteers may also feel awkward, frustrated, angry, or inadequate if the person they are working with fails to respond positively or appreciatively. On the other hand, many people discover skills and talents they never knew they possessed.

7 For many Canadians, the most difficult part of volunteering is deciding what type of volunteer work to do and what cause or organization to work for. Volunteer centres can help volunteers determine their interests and skills, and match them with one or a number of volunteer placements. Talking to friends and relatives is another excellent way to find out what you would like to do.

8 The world now offers us many opportunities to help others. Volunteers not only help improve the lives of others, they also discover a wealth of untapped potential within themselves. We will never be able to meet all the needs existing throughout the world, but, by volunteering, we can make a real difference in the lives of at least some of those in need.

# II. Responding to the Article

## A. Journal Writing and Discussion

Spend the next 10 to 15 minutes writing in your journal about anything that interests you about the article. For example, your writing might include questions about information contained in the selection, or you may want to write about points made in the article with which you agree or disagree. When you have finished, form a group with two or three other people and read your responses to each other.

## B. Finding the Main Ideas

Remain in your groups. Discuss what you think are the main ideas that the author is trying to present. You may want to elect one person as "secretary" to write down the group's ideas. Be prepared to share your ideas with the rest of the class.

# III. Comprehension Check

## A. Questions

**Part 1:** Work with members of your group to answer the following questions.

1. What are some benefits of doing volunteer work?
2. What are some of the challenges volunteers face in their work?
3. What can people do if they want to volunteer but are not sure what they want to do?
4. What are some of the areas that volunteers can participate in?
5. Is volunteering important? Give reasons to support your answer.

**Part 2:** Working with the members of your group, create five questions of your own about the article. These questions can be about specific ideas or information contained in the article, or about the meanings of particular words or phrases. When you have finished, exchange your questions with another group. Discuss the answers to the questions your group receives.

## B. True, False, and INP (Information Not Provided)

Work with a partner to complete the following exercise. Write "T" beside those sentences which are **true** and "F" beside those sentences which are **false**. Support your answer by using a sentence provided from the story. If the information in the sentence is not provided in the article, write **INP**.

1. _____ One of the most difficult parts of volunteering is deciding what type of volunteer work to do.

2. _____ Most people give up volunteering after only a few months.

3. _____ Volunteer centres can help you decide what type of volunteer work you are interested in.

4. _____ Volunteering requires that you donate a lot of time.

5. _____ Some people volunteer to meet other people.

6. _____ Most Canadian volunteers are women.

7. _____ Volunteers usually work alone.

8. _____ Volunteering is always a lot of fun.

# IV. Word Power—Synonyms

Work with a partner to complete the following exercise. Circle the letter beside the answer that gives the same meaning as the word or expression in *italics*.

1. While volunteers are needed by hundreds of organizations, *volunteering does not have to make a large demand on a person's time* (paragraph 5).
    a. Volunteering doesn't necessarily require a great deal of time.
    b. You need a lot of time to do volunteer work.
    c. Volunteering can be very time consuming.

2. Volunteers may also feel awkward, frustrated, angry, or *inadequate* if the person they are working with fails to respond positively or appreciatively (paragraph 6).
    a. annoyed
    b. delighted
    c. insufficient

3. Volunteers not only help improve the lives of others, they also discover a wealth of untapped *potential* within themselves (paragraph 8)
   a. anger
   b. talents
   c. inadequacies

4. Their efforts range from raising money to finance new hospital facilities to visiting the sick or elderly to helping feed *starving* children in developing countries (paragraph 1).
   a. malnourished
   b. illiterate
   c. unfriendly

5. A person working with a *terminally ill patient* may have to come to terms with his or her own fear of death (paragraph 6).
   a. a person who lives in a hospital
   b. a person who will be sick for a long time
   c. a person who will die because of his or her illness

# V. Active Interaction—Choosing the Volunteer of the Year

### Directions

The City of Halifax has decided to award the title of "Volunteer of the Year" to one individual for an outstanding contribution to his or her fellow citizens and community. You are a member of the city's Awards Committee which must select the Volunteer of the Year from hundreds of nominations. You have narrowed your selection down to five individuals. It is now up to your committee to select the recipient of the award. First, work on your own to rank the finalists from number one down to number five. Use the chart provided to record your selections and the reasons for them. After you have made your own personal selections, get together with two or three other committee members and compare your answers. Explain to your committee members the reasons for your choices. Your committee must come to an agreement on its choice. Use the chart provided to record your group's choices. Be prepared to share your group's decisions with other groups. Here are the finalists.

1. **Mary Clark**

Mrs. Clark is a 93-year-old volunteer at the Halifax Food Bank. She has worked eight hours a day for the past year filling grocery bags with donated food. Although the work is sometimes tiring, Mrs. Clark always has a kind word for the people she works with and the people who come to the food bank for food.

2. **Anna Sindlerova**

Ms. Sindlerova is a 25-year-old theatre student at Dalhousie University. For the past year, she has run an amateur theatre company at the local correctional facility. Twenty-five inmates are currently participating in the program. To date, the inmates have performed four plays for both the public and their fellow inmates, including works by Shakespeare and Canadian playwright Joseph Edge. In fact, several of Anna's students have gone on to professional acting careers following their release.

3. **John Marshall**

Mr. Marshall, a 75-year-old retired farmer, regularly visits elderly patients at a local nursing home. John usually goes to each of his "friends" and talks to them about their day and listens to their stories. For many, if John didn't visit them, they would rarely have visitors.

4. **Don Munroe**

Mr. Munroe is a 55-year-old house builder who for the past year has donated one weekend a month to teaching young offenders basic woodworking skills. This has allowed these young people not only to learn valuable skills but also to make important contributions to the city. For example, Don's students have constructed several children's playgrounds in local parks.

5. **Yvonne Kindred**

Ms. Kindred is a 21-year-old office worker. She is also a "Big Sister." Every weekend she spends time with a 12-year-old girl who has a mother but no father, brothers, or sisters. She takes her "little sister" on various outings including bicycle trips, the movies, and walks in the park. Mostly, however, she acts as a friend and counsellor to a needy girl.

## Choose the Volunteer of the Year

| Candidate | Your Choice | Group's Choice |
| --- | --- | --- |
| 1. Mary Clark | Final ranking ____ <br><br> Reason(s) this individual should/should not receive the award. | Final ranking ____ <br><br> Reason(s) this individual should/should not receive the reward. |
| 2. Anna Sinderlova | Final ranking ____ <br><br> Reason(s) this individual should/should not receive the award. | Final ranking ____ <br><br> Reason(s) this individual should/should not receive the award. |

Read On Canada

_____    _____
_____    _____
_____    _____
_____    _____

3. John Marshall

Final ranking ____    Final ranking ____

Reason(s) this individual should/should not receive the award.    Reason(s) this individual should/should not receive the award.

_____    _____
_____    _____
_____    _____
_____    _____
_____    _____
_____    _____
_____    _____

4. Don Munroe

Final ranking ____    Final ranking ____

Reason(s) this individual should/should not receive the award.    Reason(s) this individual should/should not receive the award.

_____    _____
_____    _____
_____    _____
_____    _____
_____    _____
_____    _____
_____    _____

5. Yvonne Kindred

Final ranking ____    Final ranking ____

Reason(s) this individual should/should not receive the award.    Reason(s) this individual should/should not receive the award.

_____    _____
_____    _____
_____    _____
_____    _____
_____    _____
_____    _____
_____    _____

# VI. Further Topics for Discussion and Composition

1. You have been asked to recruit volunteers to help run a multicultural fair at your school. You must come up with a way to attract volunteers to help run this event. Your campaign can include such things as posters and written descriptions on the importance of helping out with this event.

2. Have you ever volunteered before? If yes, describe in detail your experience. Include a description of what you did and why you chose to do that particular type of volunteer work. If you have never volunteered, describe your ideal volunteer placement. Remember to give specific reasons for your choice.

# VII. Learning Log

Go back to your journal and spend the next few minutes recording what you have learned and experienced from this particular unit. You may use your first language if this helps you to better express more complex ideas or insights.

Read On Canada

# IV-3 Consumers Protected

## I. Pre-Reading Activities

### A. Before You Read

Before reading the article, complete the following activities with the rest of the class.

- Have you ever bought something from a store, tried to use it, and discovered that it did not work properly?
- How did you feel?
- What did you do with the item?
- Share your experience with the rest of the class.
- What do you think you will learn about in this article?

Go ahead and read the article. Try not to use your dictionary to look up unfamiliar words.

1. It's Friday night and you have just spent the last half hour hooking up your brand-new CD player. You insert your favourite CD, push the play button, and an ear-wrenching, grinding sound has you scrambling for the off switch. Something is dreadfully wrong with your new equipment.

2. It happens to all of us at one time or another. The pleasure and excitement of a new purchase is replaced by anger and frustration when we realize that we have bought a defective product. There is no need to panic, however. You can get your money back, have

the item replaced or repaired, and even get compensation for any extra damage you may have suffered. The key, however, is knowing what steps to take.

3 Your first step is to take the defective item back to the seller as quickly as possible. The longer you keep a product, the greater the chance that you will lose your right to a refund or compensation. When you go back to the seller, make sure you take your sales slip, warranty card, or any other relevant documents with you. These items are essential in helping you to solve a problem. If you are uncertain or afraid about returning a product, you can always take a friend to give you a little extra confidence. Your friend can also act as a witness to what happens when you try to return the product.[1]

4 First, try complaining to the individual who sold you the product. Explain your problem clearly, politely, and calmly, and be ready with your receipts and warranties if asked. You may have to be a little persistent. Moreover, don't apologize for your actions. It's your right as a consumer to complain about faulty merchandise. Sometimes a seller can be difficult and may try to blame you for causing the problem. In most instances, however, your problem will be solved quickly because reputable dealers want to keep you as a customer. They are also aware that if they give good service you are likely to refer your friends and acquaintances to the store. You may also be helping the store—if your CD player is one of a number of similarly defective units, the sooner the store knows about the problems, the sooner they can remove or repair the items before any more are sold.

5 In many stores, particularly large department stores, the person who sold you an item does not have the power to solve your problem. In that case, you may be directed to the company's customer service department. If no such service exists, you can ask to see the store manager. If after speaking with customer service or the store manager you are still not satisfied, you can take further action. For example, you can write a complaint letter to the company president, the manufacturer, or regional distributor. Include in your complaint letter copies (not originals) of all relevant documents, including the sales slip and warranty card. Also include the date of purchase, the name of the company that sold you the product, whether you paid by cash, cheque, or credit card, what action you have taken so far, and what the company can do to solve the problem.[2]

6 If the above actions fail, you can contact your local consumer protection group for advice on what to do next. For example, they may suggest that you try mediation. In mediation, an impartial third person, a mediator, will sit down with both sides in a dispute and try to work out an agreement. Mediation is an effective approach because it is usually inexpensive and can often resolve a dispute after only one session.[3] Decisions made by a mediator, however, are not legally binding, and neither the seller nor the buyer has to abide by the decision of the mediator. Mediation services are available in many communities. Just check your local phone book. In addition to contacting a mediation service, you can call your provincial government consumer services branch. Officials can offer advice on how to handle your complaint and can also act as mediators.

7 Another approach to solving your problem is to contact your local newspaper. Many of Canada's large daily papers have consumer advice columns that provide information on a wide variety of consumer issues.

8 Contacting your local office of the Better Business Bureau is another approach in helping you to solve a dispute with a seller. The Better Business Bureau is an non-profit organization funded by local businesses to promote honesty and fair play in the marketplace. The Better Business Bureau can act as a mediator between a customer and a member company. The Better Business Bureau, however, has no authority to force a business into mediation. As with any mediation, both the buyer and the seller must be willing to participate for mediation to take place. However, it is not in the best interests of a company to ignore reasonable complaints. The Better Business Bureau keeps records of complaints against a company, and no company wants complaints to accumulate in the bureau's files. This is particularly true in that the Better Business Bureau can publicize these complaints, either in a bulletin to other member businesses or to the news media by way of a news release. The Better Business Bureau can also suggest to newspapers, magazines, or any other media that it would be in the public's best interest if they refused to carry the advertisements for a particular company until it has settled all outstanding disputes.[4]

9 If all the above procedures fail to solve your problem, you can take your case to Small Claims Court. In Small Claims Court, you can represent yourself so you don't need a lawyer. The amount of money you can sue a person for in Small Claims Court varies from province to province but in British Columbia, for instance, you can be granted a settlement of up to $10 000. To find out how to begin a small claims case against a company, check the blue pages of your phone book under "Government Court Services," or contact your local provincial court office.

10 Once your case goes to Small Claims Court, you will be required to attend a settlement conference to see if your dispute can be resolved before seeing a judge. If no settlement is reached, both the customer and the seller will go before a judge and tell their sides of the story. After hearing both sides, a judge will usually make a decision quickly.

11 The best way, however, to lessen your chances of buying a defective product or of having difficulties when trying to return an item is to be an informed and responsible consumer. Compare products and prices before buying. As well, product information is available in books and magazines such as *Consumer Reports, Canadian Consumer, Protect Yourself,* and the *Lemon Aid* car buying guides. Also, make sure you know what the product's warranty or guarantee means by asking questions before you purchase the item.

12 Remember, you have a responsibility to let other consumers know about any unfair treatment you may have received from a company. Moreover, you have the right to complain if something goes wrong.

# II. Responding to the Article

## A. Journal Writing and Discussion

Spend the next 10 to 15 minutes writing in your journal about anything that interests you about the article. For example, your writing might include questions about information contained in the selection, or you may want to write about points made in the article with which you agree or disagree. When you have finished, form a group with two or three other people and read your responses to each other.

## B. Finding the Main Ideas

Remain in your groups. Discuss what you think are the main ideas that the author is trying to present. You may want to elect one person as "secretary" to write down the group's ideas. Be prepared to share your ideas with the rest of the class.

# III. Comprehension Check

## A. Questions

**Part 1:** Work with members of your group to answer the following questions.

1. What is Small Claims Court?
2. When you return a defective product to a store, what should you bring with you?
3. What services does the Better Business Bureau provide?
4. What are mediators and what is their role?
5. Why do people sometimes not bother to return a defective product?

**Part 2:** Working with the members of your group, create five questions about the article. These questions can be about specific ideas or information contained in the article, or about the meanings of particular words or phrases. When you have finished, exchange your questions with another group. Discuss the answers to the questions your group receives.

## B. True, False, and INP (Information Not Provided)

Work with a partner to complete the following exercise. Write "T" beside those sentences which are **true** and "F" beside those sentences which are **false**. Support your answer by using a sentence provided from the story. If the information in the sentence is not provided in the article, write **INP**.

1. _____ If you buy a defective product, there is nothing you can do.

2. _____ A mediator can impose a settlement on a dealer.

3. _____ Mediation is possible without the agreement of both parties.

4. _____ The Consumer Protection Act protects most consumers.

5. _____ When returning a product you should be prepared to get angry.

6. _____ If a store gives you good service you are likely to refer other people to it.

7. _____ It is important that you know your options when returning a product.

8. _____ Product information is available in a number of publications.

9. _____ Most CD players are free of defects.

10. _____ You must bring a lawyer with you to Small Claims Court.

# IV. Word Power—Cloze Encounters

Work with a partner to complete the following exercise. Write the correct word in each of the sentences below. You can use each word only once.

| essential | publicize | abide | defective |
| relevant | refund | product | persistent |
| merchandise | conference | impartial | distributor |
| mediation | reputable | lawyer | ignore |

1. Most _____ dealers will help resolve a customer's complaint about a product.

2. The parties involved in mediation do not have to _____ by the decision of a mediator.

3. It is not in a company's best interest to _____ a complaint.

4. If you purchase a _____ product, you have the right to a refund or compensation.

5. A mediator is an _____ third party in a dispute.

6. You can sometimes _____ your complaint in the local newspaper.

7. You do not have to bring a _____ to Small Claims Court.

8. Before going to court, you will be asked to participate in a settlement _____.

9. When returning a product, you sometimes have to be _____ .

10. Before purchasing any _____, find out as much information as you can about the product.

# V. Active Interaction—Faulty Merchandise Role-Play

**Direction**

For this role-play activity, you will be working together with a partner. To begin, one partner will read and act out the role described in Student A—Part I: The Dissatisfied Customer while the other partner reads and acts out the role described in Student B—Part I: The Customer Service Agent. Be prepared to present your role-play to the rest of the class. When you have finished this activity, Student A will then play the role described in Student A—Part II: The Customer Service Agent while Student B acts out the role described in Student B—Part II: The Dissatisfied Customer.

**Customer Complaint A**

**Part I:** *The Dissatisfied Customer*

You have just bought a couple of items from a local department store. Unfortunately, neither works properly. The first item is a CD player that plays all your CDs backwards. The other item is a computer that suddenly stops working, usually when you are trying to do important work. Pretend that you are returning the items to the store. Describe the problems to the customer service agent and try to come up with a solution to your problems.

**Part II:** *The Customer Service Agent*

A customer will try to get his money back for a camera he bought. Unfortunately, the sales contract says that he can only exchange the item for another camera of equal value. Try to work out a solution that satisfies you both.

**Customer Complaint B**

**Part I:** *Customer Service Agent*

A customer has just brought two items back to the store. The customer claims that the items are not working properly. Your store has never had a problem with these goods and you suspect that the customer is responsible for the damage. Good customer relations are important to you, but you want to find the truth. After discussing the problems with the customer, try to come up with a solution that satisfies you both.

**Part II:** *The Dissatisfied Customer*

You just bought a new and very expensive camera from your local camera store to take on your trip to Hawaii. While on your trip, the camera lens fell off and smashed on the ground. You have now returned from your trip. You just want your money back and you are not interested in buying another camera from this particular store.

# VI. Further Topics for Discussion and Composition

1. You have discovered that the new cellular telephone you just bought is not working properly. You take the phone back to the store, but the salesperson refuses to replace it or fix it for free. When you ask to see the manager, she says she doesn't want to talk to you. Write a complaint letter to the Better Business Bureau describing your problem.

2. Describe an instance when you had to return something to a store. Describe in detail exactly what happened and how the experience made you feel.

3. Your grandmother, who does not understand English very well, thought that she was simply receiving a gift when in fact she was ordering a freezer full of beef from a telephone solicitor. When the meat arrives, she wants to send it back, but the delivery people say it cannot be returned because it is a custom order. What should she do?

# VII. Learning Log

Go back to your journal and spend the next few minutes recording what you have learned and experienced from this particular unit. You may use your first language if this helps you to better express more complex ideas or insights.

## Word List: Crossword puzzle

| | | |
|---|---|---|
| COMPASSIONATE | GRAFFITI | RACISM |
| COMPENSATION | GRIEVANCE | REFUGEE |
| CREED | IGNORE | REFUND |
| DEMAND | INADEQUATE | RELIGIOUS |
| DISPENSABLE | LAWYER | REPUTABLE |
| ESSENTIAL | MEDIATION | UNTAPPED |
| FAMINE | PROMOTION | VOLUNTEERS |

# Crossword Puzzle

**Across**

1. Organizations, like the Red Cross, depend heavily on the work of _____.
3. It is extremely difficult to simply _____ acts of racism.
6. Volunteers can sometimes feel awkward, frustrated, or _____.
9. A person convicted of racial harassment may have to pay _____.
10. A great shortage of food in a country or area is called a _____.
15. A _____ is someone who leaves one place to find safety in another.
16. Many immigrant women work in low-paying _____ jobs.
18. _____ is a belief that some races are better than others.
19. People often discover _____ potential when volunteering.
20. A person's _____ can be described as someone's religious beliefs.

**Down**

2. Sometimes consumer complaints go to _____.
4. A victim of racism can file a _____ against the offender.
5. Most people don't need a _____ to settle consumer complaints.
7. Many Canadians volunteer for _____ organizations.
8. If you are dissatisfied with a product, many stores will simply _____ your money.
9. Canadians like to think of themselves as a caring and _____ people.
11. When making a complaint have all the _____ information with you.
12. Racist _____ was spray-painted on the building.
13. The worker felt she did not receive the _____ because of her colour.
14. It's always best to shop at a _____ dealer.
17. Being a volunteer does not have to make a big _____ on your time.

Courtesy of the Department of National Defence

# Chapter V

# CANADA IN THE GLOBAL VILLAGE

*Canada and the Global Village*

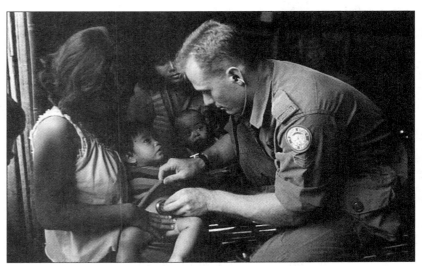

Photos courtesy of the Department of National Defence

Read On Canada

# V-1 The Reconciliation: Canada's UN Peacekeepers

## I. Pre-Reading Activities

### A. Before You Read

Before reading the article, complete the following activities with the rest of the class.

- Look at page 105.
- Who are the people in the pictures?
- What is happening?
- Where in the world do you think these people are?
- Share your ideas with the rest of the class.
- What do you think you will learn about in this article?

Go ahead and read the article. Try not to use your dictionary to look up unfamiliar words.

1 One of the major goals of Canadian foreign policy is to help resolve armed conflict peacefully wherever it occurs around the world. One of the most successful ways Canada accomplishes this goal is by participating in United Nations-sponsored peacekeeping missions.

2 Since 1947, more than ninety thousand Canadians have served under the UN flag.[1] In fact, Canada's participation in United Nations peacekeeping efforts is unparalleled. However, we have also paid a price for this commitment to peace. Almost 400 Canadian soldiers have been killed while trying to stop the suffering of war.[2]

3 One of Canada's first peacekeeping missions took place in Kashmir in 1949. Twenty-seven personnel were sent to the area to observe a cease-fire between Indian and Pakistani troops.[3] Both countries had fought bitterly for control of the territory. Besides monitoring the cease-fire, Canadian observers were also required to make sure that neither army moved their troops to try to gain an advantage. In short, the peacekeepers tried to get everyone to calm down while diplomats worked to find a permanent solution to the problem. Canada has since played a similar role many times in places such as West New Guinea (1962-63), Yemen (1963-64), and, more recently, in Afghanistan (1988-90) and the former Yugoslavia (1992- ).[4]

4 Besides acting as observers, Canadian peacekeepers have set up buffer zones to keep warring groups apart. The first example of this interposition role occurred during the Suez Crisis. In 1956, Britain, France, and Israel joined forces to attack Egypt. They were

trying to get control of the Suez Canal, an important economic and commercial waterway. In response, Canada's Secretary of State, Lester B. Pearson, helped establish the first formal UN peacekeeping force called the United Nations Emergency Force. The primary role of UNEF I was to stand between Egypt and Israel in the Sinai desert. At first, the Egyptian leader, Gamal Abdel Nasser, did not want the Canadians to participate in the UN force. At that time, Canadian soldiers wore similar uniforms to the British, Egypt's enemy.* To help solve this problem, thousands of old American army helmet liners were spray-painted light blue to match the colour of the UN flag. Ever since, the blue helmets (and blue berets) have been the symbol of United Nations peacekeepers.[5]

5  Since the Suez Crisis, Canada has helped to keep enemies apart many times. For example, after leaving the Sinai in 1967, Canada was asked to return to help keep the peace between Egypt and Israel from 1973 to the present. Canada has also sent troops to such places as Lebanon (1958-59 and 1978), Syria (1974- ), the border between Iran and Iraq (1988-91), and Somalia (1992- ).[6]

6  Peacekeeping can be an extremely dangerous mission. One of the main jobs given to Canadian peacekeepers in countries such as Cambodia and the former Yugoslavia is to find and destroy land mines, booby traps, and other unexploded bombs.[7] In addition, the peacekeepers must teach local people to identify and avoid these weapons. For example, in Kuwait, one Canadian soldier was horrified when children began bringing in live land mines for the UN troops to dispose of.[8] Canadian soldiers are also asked to patrol borders and to maintain law and order, often while being shot at by snipers. Furthermore, with each new mission, Canadians are asked to perform more and more complex duties which are outside their traditional peacekeeping role. These include monitoring elections, distributing food aid, and providing emergency medical assistance. In addition, United Nations forces used to enter an area only after a cease-fire had been put in place. Canadians, however, are increasingly being asked to begin their peacekeeping duties before the shooting has stopped.

7  Canadian troops also face many dangers from nature. For example, in the Golan Heights troops must watch out for large poisonous snakes, such as the Palestinian Viper, as well as black rat snakes and scorpions.[9] In Asia, soldiers must protect themselves from a variety of tropical diseases such as malaria.

8  While the presence of Canadians troops has helped save many lives, peacekeeping can still be extremely frustrating. For instance, Canadian troops have been stationed on Cyprus since 1974. The Greek and Turkish Cypriot communities, however, are still a long way from finding a permanent solution to their dispute over ownership of the island.[10] Canada also faced difficulties in Vietnam in 1973. At that time, peacekeeping forces from Poland and Hungary (both Communist countries then) began helping North Vietnam, another Communist country, rather than remaining neutral as peacekeepers are supposed to.[11] However, it was also alleged that Canada was openly siding with the South Vietnamese.

---

* Canada also agreed not to deploy an infantry battalion called The Queen's Own Rifles of Canada as this would have only added to Egypt's perception that Canada might not be entirely neutral in the Suez conflict.

9 Perhaps the proudest moment for Canadian peacekeepers came in 1988. In that year the "blue helmets" were awarded the Nobel Peace Prize in recognition of their contributions to maintaining world peace. In addition, on October 8, 1992, a monument to Canadian peacekeepers was unveiled near Parliament Hill in Ottawa. It was called *The Reconciliation* to honour the sacrifice and courage of our UN forces.[12] As long as support for peacekeeping missions continues in Canada, our forces will continue to help create an environment in which a peaceful solution to problems can take place.

*The Reconciliation in Ottawa.*
Courtesy of the Department of National Defence

# II. Responding to the Article

## A. Journal Writing and Discussion

Spend the next 10 to 15 minutes writing in your journal about anything that interests you about the article. For example, your writing might include questions about information contained in the selection, or you may want to write about points made in the article with which you agree or disagree. When you have finished, form a group with two or three other people and read your responses to each other.

## B. Finding the Main Ideas

Remain in your groups. Discuss what you think are the main ideas that the author is trying to present. You may want to elect one person as "secretary" to write down the group's ideas. Be prepared to share your ideas with the rest of the class.

# III. Comprehension Check

## A. Questions

**Part 1:** Work with members of your group to answer the following questions.

1. Why are UN peacekeeping helmets and berets light blue in colour?
2. Describe some of the ways that peacekeeping can be dangerous.
3. What difficulties did Canadian peacekeepers experience in Vietnam in 1973?
4. What are some of the duties that Canadian peacekeepers are expected to perform?
5. What is *The Reconciliation* and why was it built?

**Part 2:** Working with the members of your group, create five questions about the article. These questions can be about specific ideas or information contained in the article, or about the meanings of particular words or phrases. When you have finished, exchange your questions with another group. Discuss the answers to the questions your group receives.

## B. True, False, and INP (Information Not Provided)

Work with a partner to complete the following exercise. Write "T" beside those sentences which are **true** and "F" beside those sentences which are **false**. Support your answer by using a sentence provided from the story. If the information in the sentence is not provided in the article, write **INP**.

1. \_\_\_\_\_ Canada's first peacekeeping mission occurred in 1974.

2. \_\_\_\_\_ Peacekeepers set up buffer zones to keep warring groups apart.

3. \_\_\_\_\_ *The Reconciliation* was unveiled on October 8, 1992.

4. \_\_\_\_\_ Lester B. Pearson was Prime Minister of Canada when UNEF I was established.

5. \_\_\_\_\_ Peacekeepers' helmets are light blue in colour.

6. \_\_\_\_\_ Canada currently has peacekeeping troops in Germany.

7. \_\_\_\_\_ UN peacekeepers were awarded the Nobel Peace Prize.

8. \_\_\_\_\_ Peacekeeping is rarely a hazardous job.

# IV. Word Power—Antonyms

Work with a partner to complete the exercise on the following page. From the list on the left, choose a word with the *opposite* meaning from the list on the right.

1. neutral
2. frustrating
3. patrol
4. famine
5. solution
6. sufficient
7. permanent
8. participate
9. cease-fire
10. impose
11. calm
12. live

a. _____ abundance
b. _____ biased
c. _____ war
d. _____ abstain
e. _____ inactive
f. _____ inadequate
g. _____ satisfying
h. _____ temporary
i. _____ problem
j. _____ remove

# V. Active Interaction—Should Canada Continue to Send Peacekeepers to Other Countries?

**Directions**

Below are some of the arguments for and against Canada's involvement in UN peacekeeping missions. With a partner or in a small group, rank these statements in terms of how much you agree or disagree with them. Rank the statement you agree with most as number 1 and the statement you disagree with most as number 10. When you have finished, compare your answers with your classmates'. Be prepared to give reasons for your choices.

a. _____ Canada provides 10 percent of the world's peacekeepers, but makes up only 0.5 percent of the world's population and has the world's hundredth largest army. It's time that other UN members did more of the work.

b. _____ Canada must continue to be involved in peacekeeping missions. Canadians have been doing peacekeeping missions longer than anyone else and are considered the world's best peacekeepers.

c. _____ With Canadian governments continuing to cut the military budget, money spent on peacekeeping limits the regular army's capability to engage in combat anywhere in the world.

d. _____ Canada should continue its involvement in UN peacekeeping missions because peacekeeping is critical for preventing small local conflicts from expanding into wider wars.

e. _____ UN peacekeeping missions are becoming too dangerous. Soldiers are increasingly being asked to begin peacekeeping duties before a cease-fire has been established.

f. _____ Canadians are becoming increasingly reluctant to send soldiers to risk their lives in foreign conflicts.

g. _____ The best way to defend Canada is to keep the peace abroad.

h. _____ Peacekeeping often only stops two groups from fighting but does nothing to resolve the real problems.

i. _____ Instead of sending its soldiers on peacekeeping missions, Canada should keep its armed forces at home for use in air/sea rescue and for patrolling our 200-mile limit in territorial waters.

j. _____ Peacekeeping is no longer an effective way to solve problems. In some countries, there is no regular government authority but a mishmash of irregular bands of soldiers terrorizing the population. There is no one with whom a peacekeeping force can come to an agreement.

# VI. Further Topics for Discussion and Composition

1. Do you think Canada should continue to play a major role in international peacekeeping even though it is expensive and increasingly dangerous? Give specific reasons for your answer.

2. Pretend that you are the head of a Canadian peacekeeping force. You have just entered a small town that has been devastated by a recent attack. Many people are injured and there are limited supplies of food and water. How would you go about helping the local people? What jobs could you ask different members of your force to do?

3. You are writing an article for your school newspaper about a graduate from your school who has just returned from a peacekeeping mission in Somalia. Prepare a list of questions to ask him or her during the interview.

# VII. Learning Log

Go back to your journal and spend the next few minutes recording what you have learned and experienced from this particular unit. You may use your first language if this helps you to better express your complex ideas or insights.

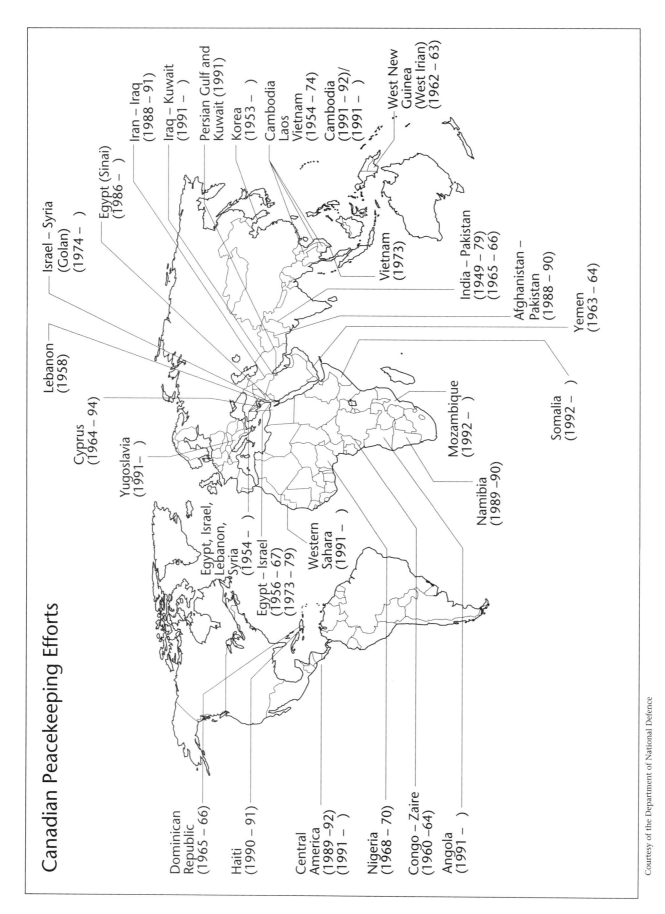

*Canada and the Global Village*

# V-2 Helping People to Help Themselves: OXFAM-Canada

## I. Pre-Reading Activities

*Jobs in Afta, Eritrea. Gemia Ahmed speaks out about the need for women to take part in the fisheries development program supported by OXFAM-Canada.*
Courtesy OXFAM-Canada

*A clinic in Esteli, Nicaragua. OXFAM-Canada gives money to health care projects such as this one, run by the Farm Workers Union (ATC).*
Courtesy OXFAM-Canada

*A community group builds peace, justice, and democracy in Quiche, Guatemala. The Ixcan Grande Cooperative, supported by OXFAM-Canada, is made up of some of the tens of thousands who fled massacres of Mayans by the Guatemala army in 1982.*
Courtesy OXFAM-Canada

### A. Before You Read

Before reading the article, complete the following activities with the rest of the class.

- What do the words "starvation," "famine," and "malnutrition" mean?
- Make a list of all the words you associate with these words.
- What do you think are the causes of world hunger?
- How can we prevent hunger and starvation?
- What are the names of three countries that have been stricken by starvation in the last ten years?
- Locate them on a map.
- What do you think you will learn about in this article?

Go ahead and read the article. Try to guess the meaning of words that are unfamiliar to you.

1. Every year, throughout the world, more than 500 million people die from the effects of hunger and malnutrition. That figure includes nearly 13 million children who die before they reach the age of five. In addition, at least 900 million people, nearly one-fifth of the world's population, are undernourished.[1]

2. While the causes of hunger include war and natural disasters such as floods and drought, hunger is primarily the result of poverty. Poor people tend to be hungry because they lack the resources to grow enough food for themselves or the money to buy it. Malnutrition in turn makes them more susceptible to diseases such as polio and tuberculosis. Consequently, they are less able to work and earn an income or to sustain themselves during food shortages. The poor, too, usually live in inadequate housing and have few employment or educational opportunities.

3. One Canadian volunteer organization that seeks to address the causes of poverty is OXFAM-Canada. Established in 1963, OXFAM-Canada is an independent member of an international association of OXFAM organizations located in various parts of the world. It is funded by grants from the Canadian International Development Agency (CIDA) as well as by private donations.

4. One of OXFAM-Canada's primary objectives is to fund projects initiated by community groups in Africa, Central America, and the Caribbean. These organizations, which OXFAM calls "project partners," are seeking to better the quality of life of poor people through improved basic health care, self-sufficiency in food production, and education. For example, in Ethiopia, OXFAM-Canada is funding a project established in cooperation with the Relief Society of Tigre to restore unproductive farmland damaged by overuse, erosion, and war. This project also involves establishing seed banks to provide seeds to loan to farmers. In Zimbabwe, OXFAM-Canada funds the Rural Association for Progress (ORAP). ORAP assists over 450 community groups with development projects in food production, storage, and distribution. These groups also dig wells, set up libraries, and build houses and schools. The net result of these programs has been to help peasant farmers in Zimbabwe double their food production in just over ten years.

5. OXFAM-Canada also works with local farmers by sponsoring initiatives such as the Campesino to Campesino project in Nicaragua. One of the goals of this program is to develop ways to grow food that do not harm the environment and which allow farmers to produce food in the same areas year after year. In many parts of the world, farmers have become dependent on chemical fertilizers and pesticides to grow crops. These chemicals are expensive and pollute local water supplies. When farmers can no longer afford these chemicals, they often lack the knowledge and skills to keep the land productive using traditional farming methods. As a result, nutrients in the soil are quickly used up and the land can no longer be used to grow food. The Campesino to Campesino program stresses the use of traditional soil and water conservation techniques as well as the use of natural fertilizers. This program has helped to lower the cost of food production and decreased the need to buy expensive imported food.

6. In addition to supporting projects that help people to grow their own food, OXFAM-Canada has established a trading company known as Bridgehead. This company is part

of an international group of trading organizations that seek to promote fair trade between rich and poor nations. Working mostly with cooperatives, Bridgehead imports hand-crafted gifts and food from groups that would otherwise be too small to export on their own. In turn, many of these cooperatives use their profits to fund social programs in their communities such as health care, education, and literacy classes. When choosing products, Bridgehead also looks at what impact they have on the environment and on worker health and safety. Bridgehead also chooses products that reflect the cultures of its project partners and that help preserve traditional skills and art forms.

7 Land redistribution and restoration are other important aspects of OXFAM-Canada's work. In many countries, the majority of the land is owned and controlled by a minority of the population. Often landowners use this land to grow only "cash crops" such as cotton, sugar cane, and coffee, and not to grow food for the local people. A large amount of land is also used to raise beef that is sold to the United States and Canada. Therefore, OXFAM-Canada is working with groups such as the Association for Inter-Community Health and Social Services (APSIES) in El Salvador who want families to get a fair share of the land and the food security it brings. OXFAM-Canada is also working in partnership with the Transvaal Rural Action Centre (TRAC) in South Africa. TRAC is working for the return of land forcibly taken from the local people under the former government's apartheid program.

8 Another important part of OXFAM-Canada's work is in the area of human rights. OXFAM supports labour organizations and unions that are struggling to improve the wages and working conditions of workers employed by foreign-owned companies. Also, in countries like El Salvador and Guatemala, people working for social change are often harassed and murdered. Consequently, OXFAM-Canada is working with local human rights organizations to help protect these individuals.

9 Because of recurring incidents of famine, drought, and war, many people living in poverty also lack basic health care. For example, in Eritrea, many women suffer a tremendous number of health problems as the result of malnutrition and unsanitary conditions while giving birth. They also have little education or training in prenatal and postnatal care. To address this need, OXFAM-Canada is funding a project organized and operated by the National Union of Eritrean Women to train more than 320 midwives per year. This ten-week program provides these birth attendants with information on nutrition and hygiene, as well as on prenatal and postnatal care. This program has not only helped to bring primary health care to women living in remote areas, it has dramatically decreased the death rate among mothers and children.

10 The AIDS epidemic is having a devastating impact everywhere, but particularly in Africa. In response, OXFAM-Canada directly supports local AIDS awareness and education projects established by local AIDS service organizations in Zimbabwe, Namibia, and South Africa, as well as in Canada. OXFAM-Canada also supports popular educational theatre groups such as Puppets Against AIDS that has toured not only throughout Africa but also in Canada.

*This group from South Africa, supported by OXFAM-Canada, came to Canada to teach Canadians about the use of puppetry in health education.*
Courtesy OXFAM-Canada

11 In addition to supporting health care education programs, OXFAM-Canada sponsors programs that teach people to read and write. In Jamaica, for example, OXFAM-Canada is working with the Women's Resource and Outreach Centre to provide literacy programs as well as sewing skills. These skills help people to set up and manage their own businesses, establish bank accounts, and become more self-reliant.

12 OXFAM-Canada recognizes that the causes and impacts of poverty are the same, whether in the developing world or here in Canada. As a result, OXFAM-Canada's Domestic Program helps organize a number of linkage programs that provide opportunities for workers, health care professionals, and Aboriginal peoples to get together to discuss issues of common concern. For example, OXFAM-Canada sponsored a round table on Aboriginal issues. The round table provided an opportunity for representatives of Aboriginal organizations, churches, and international organizations from all over the world to meet and discuss issues such as land claims, environmental destruction, and resource management.

13 While OXFAM-Canada has worked successfully to support development projects that help to relieve poverty, much work remains to be done. The economic gap between rich and poor countries continues to expand, with nearly one quarter of the world's population living in poverty. Unless governments and the people in both rich and poor nations make a meaningful attempt to make significant economic and social changes, poverty and the tremendous suffering it causes will only worsen.

# II. Responding to the Article

## A. Journal Writing and Discussion

Spend the next 10 to 15 minutes writing in your journal about anything that interests you about the article. For example, your writing might include questions about information contained in the selection, or you may want to write about points made in the article with which you agree or disagree. When you have finished, form a group with two or three other people and read your responses to each other.

## B. Finding the Main Ideas

Remain in your groups. Discuss what you think are the main ideas that the author is trying to present. You may want to elect one person as "secretary" to write down the group's ideas. Be prepared to share your ideas with the rest of the class.

# III. Comprehension Check

## A. Questions

**Part 1:** Work with members of your group to answer the following questions.

1. Why should Canadians worry about problems so far away?
2. What is Bridgehead?
3. How does OXFAM help relieve the causes of poverty?
4. What is a midwife?
5. Why is land distribution important if people are going to feed themselves?

**Part 2:** Working with the members of your group, create five questions of your own about the article. These questions can be about specific ideas or information contained in the article, or about the meaning of particular words or phrases. When you have finished, exchange your questions with another group. Discuss the answers to the questions your group receives.

## B. True, False, and INP (Information Not Provided)

Work with a partner to complete the following exercise. Write "T" beside those sentences which are **true** and "F" beside those sentences which are **false**. Support your answer by using a sentence provided from the story. If the information in the sentence is not provided in the article, write **INP**.

1. _____ Nearly one-fifth of the world's population is undernourished.

2. _____ OXFAM-Canada is funded only by the federal government.

3. _____ OXFAM-Canada wants developing countries to become dependent on its aid programs.

4. _____ OXFAM-Canada supports programs that help protect human rights.

5. _____ Hunger and malnutrition are primarily the result of poverty.

6. _____ OXFAM-Canada opposes armed conflict.

# IV. Word Power—Word Forms

In the sentences below, choose the correct form of the word.

| Noun | Verb | Adjective | Adverb |
|---|---|---|---|
| malnutrition | | malnourished | |
| restoration | restore | restored | |
| erosion | erode | eroded | |
| sanitation | | sanitary | |
| poverty | impoverish | impoverished | |
| force | force | forced/ forcible | forcibly |
| expansion | expand | expansive | expansively |
| murderer | murder | murderous | murderously |

1. Some governments _____ citizens who oppose them.
2. _____ can occur from eating too little food or from eating poor quality food..
3. Many children live and play in extremely _____ conditions.
4. _____ is the main cause of hunger in the world.
5. Poor farming techniques can encourage soil _____ .

# V. Active Interaction—Fund-raising for a Good Cause

This activity works best with groups of four to five. Your group has decided to raise money for one of the following projects:

- a seed bank in Tigre
- the Campesino to Campesino program in Nicaragua
- the midwife-training program in Eritrea
- a literacy program in Jamaica
- a school library project in South Africa
- an AIDS awareness project in Vancouver
- any other similar project that interests you

Now you must decide how to raise money. You know that to get people to give away or donate some money, you have to both grab their interest and convince them that your cause is a good one. Often, simply having a good cause is not enough. You need to find a fund-raising activity that is fun and creative to get people's attention.

Write a fund-raising plan that includes the following information. Include samples of your media materials.

- Where will the money go? You may need to do some research in the library to be able to talk about "your" project—where it is located, what kind of area it is in, etc.
- Why should people donate some of their money to this cause? Why is it important?
- How will you get people's attention? Television and radio ads, posters, flyers, newsletters, videos, speakers, plays, songs, t-shirts... Design some sample materials to go with your plan.
- Will you ask people simply to donate money or will you sell something, collect something, or stage a special event? (Explain in detail.)
- How much money do you think you could raise using this plan?
- Why not consider putting this plan into action? All it takes to help raise money for a non-profit organization is some time and a lot of enthusiasm.

# VI. Further Topics for Discussion and Composition

1. Many developing countries spend millions of dollars each year to buy weapons for their armies instead of helping their people to grow food. Imagine a world in which weapons have not been invented. How would the world be different? What would governments do with all that money? How would people solve disagreements? Write an essay outlining some of your thoughts.

2. How can food aid sometimes hurt a developing country more than help it?

3. Beyond saving people's lives, why is it important for Canadians to support development projects overseas? What could happen if we simply ignore the problem of world hunger?

4. Do you think developing countries should take care of their own needs and not rely on others to help? Give reasons to support your answer.

5. Should money currently spent on international aid be used to help Canadians rather than other people? Give reasons to support your answer.

Read On Canada

6. Look at the chart "How We Compare: World Assistance to Developing Countries." How does Canada compare to the other nations listed when it comes to providing help to other countries? What factors do you think determine how much assistance a country gives to other countries?

## How We Compare: World Assistance to Developing Countries
(All figures in millions of U.S. dollars; circles represent 1 percent of GNP*.)

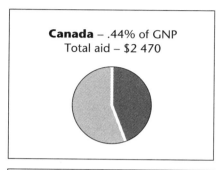

**Canada** – .44% of GNP
Total aid – $2 470

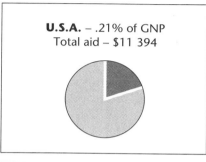

**U.S.A.** – .21% of GNP
Total aid – $11 394

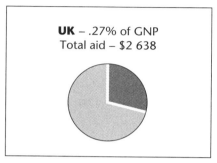

**UK** – .27% of GNP
Total aid – $2 638

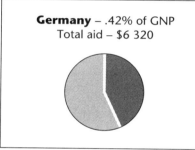

**Germany** – .42% of GNP
Total aid – $6 320

**Sweden** – .90% of GNP
Total aid – $2 012

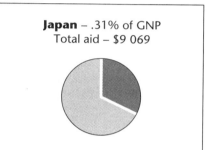

**Japan** – .31% of GNP
Total aid – $9 069

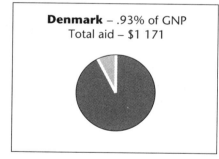

**Denmark** – .93% of GNP
Total aid – $1 171

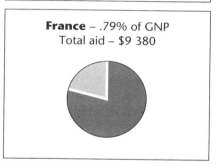

**France** – .79% of GNP
Total aid – $9 380

*GNP = Gross National Product; total worth of all goods and services usually produced in a single year.
Source: *Canadian Global Almanac, 1994.* Statistics are for 1990.

# VII. Learning Log

Go back to your journal and spend the next few minutes recording what you have learned and experienced from this particular unit. You may use your first language if this helps you to better express more complex ideas or insights.

*Canada and the Global Village*

# V-3 Getting Away With Murder

## I. Pre-Reading Activities

*Indigenous people in the Philippines demonstrate for their rights.*
Courtesy Amnesty International

*Other street children carry the coffin of Nahaman Carmona, killed by a death squad in Guatemala.*
Courtesy Amnesty International

### A. Before You Read

Before reading the article, complete the following activities with the rest of the class.

- What do the words "torture," "injustice," and "human rights" mean?
- Why do you think some governments use torture against their citizens?
- What is the death penalty?
- Is it an effective way to deter crime?
- What does the word "amnesty" mean?
- What do you think you will learn about in this article?

Go ahead and read the article. Try not to use your dictionary to look up unfamiliar words.

1. Each year in more than 140 countries throughout the world, thousands of ordinary men, women, and children are victims of flagrant or outright human rights violations. These violations include torture, executions, and disappearances, as well as arrest and detainment without cause. In many instances, these people were not given a trial or even charged with committing a crime. One grassroots volunteer organization that tries to help these victims of injustice is Amnesty International.

2. Amnesty International is a worldwide human rights organization made up of people from all walks of life. It has been working on behalf of victims of human rights abuses for over thirty years. It was formed in 1961 after two Portuguese students were arrested and imprisoned in Lisbon for publicly drinking a toast to freedom. Peter Beneson, a lawyer from England, was outraged by the action of the Portuguese government. He decided to develop ways to put pressure on oppressive governments to release the thousands of men and women imprisoned around the world because of their political and religious beliefs. Along with two friends, Eric Baker and Louis Blom-Cooper, Beneson began a one-year campaign called "Appeal for Amnesty 1961" to let the public know what was happening to political prisoners around the world. Thus began Amnesty International. Since 1961, Amnesty International has grown to include more than 1.1 million members in over 150 countries. In Canada alone, more than 75 000 volunteers and donors contribute to the work of Amnesty International.

3. Amnesty International's main goal is to seek the release of what it calls "prisoners of conscience." These are people who are imprisoned simply because they hold political or religious views that their governments do not agree with. These individuals may also be imprisoned because of their ethnic origins, colour, sex, or language. A prisoner of conscience is also someone who has not used and does not advocate the use of violence.

4. Amnesty International promotes the use of fair and prompt trials for all political prisoners. In addition, Amnesty International works on behalf of all prisoners who have been denied a trial or who have never been charged with a crime. Amnesty also opposes the death penalty and torture, as well as any other cruel or degrading treatment of prisoners.

5. Amnesty International carries out its mandate in a number of ways. First, Amnesty International "adopts" prisoners from all over the world. Amnesty will then do all it can to gain the release of the prisoners as well as support the prisoners' families. A prisoner is usually adopted only after a thorough investigation. Amnesty researchers collect and analyze information from a variety of sources, including the government and news media, as well as any witnesses. The researchers want to find out why a person was arrested and where that person is being kept prisoner. If they are able to establish that a prisoner is, in fact, a prisoner of conscience, the information is passed on to Amnesty groups worldwide.

6. Amnesty is impartial. That means it does not defend or oppose the beliefs of the prisoners it adopts. Nor does it support or oppose any government or political system. In addition, Amnesty does not accept any money from any government. Members do not want to be accused of working for a particular government or political organization.

7. It is wrong to assume that only military dictatorships and autocratic governments imprison, torture, and execute political prisoners. Often these terrible acts are also carried out by democratically elected governments. These governments are concerned about holding on to political power and feel threatened by anyone they think could take power away from them. Some opposition groups too are guilty of violating human rights. They sometimes

kidnap and murder government officials in an attempt to take control of the government. Amnesty opposes the actions of these groups as well.

8 One of the main international agreements that Amnesty International uses as a standard to judge the actions of governments is the Universal Declaration of Human Rights. This document outlines a basic set of principles that says that all people should be able to live in freedom, peace, and without fear. Unfortunately, while many countries in the world have signed the Universal Declaration of Human Rights, along with a number of other international agreements, many governments choose to ignore it. This includes countries such as China, Indonesia, Israel, Guatemala, Mynamar, Iran, and Iraq. The governments of these countries continue to torture and kill their citizens with complete disregard for international law. Canada, too, has been criticized by Amnesty International for violating the human rights of Aboriginal peoples.

9 The main tool used by Amnesty International to seek the release of prisoners of conscience is letter writing. Amnesty members write tens of thousands of letters every year to presidents, monarchs, generals, ambassadors, and anyone else who may be able to help. The letters may ask the individual to investigate a particular case, release a prisoner, or ensure that the government respects an individual's human rights. Writing letters puts international pressure on governments, especially when letters arrive by the thousands and come from individuals of all ages and professions from all over the world. Letters also let the government know that the world is watching and will hold the government responsible for the fate of the prisoner.

10 It is difficult to know how many prisoners are released as a result of Amnesty's letter-writing campaigns. In addition, Amnesty never takes sole credit for the release of a prisoner because many different human rights or religious groups may be working for the release of the same individual. However, many former prisoners have told Amnesty that its work has led to an improvement of their conditions and/or to their eventual release. For example, Julio de la Pena Valdez, a former prisoner of conscience in the Dominican Republic, writes:

> I was being kept naked in an underground cell. When the first two hundred letters came the guards gave me my clothes back. Then the next two hundred letters came and the prison director came to see me. When the next pile of letters arrived the director got in touch with his supervisor. The letters kept coming: three thousand of them. The president was informed. The letters still kept arriving and the president called the prison and told them to let me go.[1]

11 In addition to letter writing, people support Amnesty International in many other ways. For example, many volunteers are involved in fund-raising and publicity campaigns. A number of famous musicians have also helped to raise money for Amnesty. These include Sting, Bruce Springsteen, Soul Asylum, U2, and Tracy Chapman. Other volunteers give talks in schools, do film presentations, and put on plays.

12 If we are to protect people from governments that imprison, torture, and kill their citizens, we must act. If we allow governments to brutalize people without responding, we only encourage them to continue these crimes. Working with groups like Amnesty International gives ordinary people an opportunity to tell prisoners of conscience that they have not been forgotten and that they may someday be returned to freedom.

# II. Responding to the Article

## A. Journal Writing and Discussion

Spend the next 10 to 15 minutes writing in your journal about anything that interests you about the article. For example, your writing might include questions about information contained in the selection, or you may want to write about points made in the article with which you agree or disagree. When you have finished, form a group with two or three other people and read your responses to each other.

## B. Finding the Main Ideas

Remain in your groups. Discuss what you think are the main ideas that the author is trying to present. You may want to elect one person as "secretary" to write down the group's ideas. Be prepared to share your ideas with the rest of the class.

# III. Comprehension Check

## A. Questions

Part 1: Work with members of your group to answer the following questions.

1. What is Amnesty International?
2. What is Amnesty International's main goal?
3. What does Amnesty do to help achieve this goal?
4. Why do you think torture is still used in so many countries?
5. What can we do to discourage the use of torture around the world?

Part 2: Working with the members of your group, create five questions about the article. These questions can be about specific ideas or information contained in the article, or about the meanings of particular words or phrases. When you have finished, exchange your questions with another group. Discuss the answers to the questions your group receives.

## B. True, False, and INP (Information Not Provided)

Work with a partner to complete the following exercise. Write "T" beside those sentences which are **true** and "F" beside those sentences which are **false**. Support your answer by using a sentence provided from the article. If the information in the sentence is not provided in the article, write **INP**.

1. _____ Sometimes torture is carried out in countries that have democratically elected governments.

2. \_\_\_\_\_ Amnesty is impartial.

3. \_\_\_\_\_ The Universal Declaration of Human Rights outlines a set of principles that says that all people should live in freedom and peace, and without fear.

4. \_\_\_\_\_ The main tool used by Amnesty to seek the release of prisoners of conscience is political pressure.

5. \_\_\_\_\_ Amnesty often receives responses to its letter writing campaigns.

6. \_\_\_\_\_ Most of Amnesty's members live in Canada and the United States.

7. \_\_\_\_\_ Prisoners of conscience are never released from prison.

8. \_\_\_\_\_ Amnesty volunteers are never involved in fund-raising and publicity campaigns.

# IV. Word Power—Synonyms

Work with a partner to complete the following exercise. From the list on the left, choose a word with the *same* meaning as the word in the list on the right.

1. torture
2. analyze
3. trial
4. prompt
5. victim
6. prisoner
7. injustice
8. penalty
9. advocate
10. adopt
11. autocratic
12. criticize

a. \_\_\_\_\_ investigate
b. \_\_\_\_\_ speedy
c. \_\_\_\_\_ inmate
d. \_\_\_\_\_ unfairness
e. \_\_\_\_\_ punishment
f. \_\_\_\_\_ supporter
g. \_\_\_\_\_ dictatorial
h. \_\_\_\_\_ casualty
i. \_\_\_\_\_ litigation
j. \_\_\_\_\_ denounce

# V. Active Interaction—For or Against Torture

**Directions**

Below are some of the arguments for and against the use of torture. With a partner or in a small group, rank these arguments in terms of how much you agree or disagree with them. Rank the statement you agree with most as number 1 and the statement you disagree with most as number 9. When you have finished, compare your answers with your classmates. Be prepared to give reasons for your choices.

a. _____ Terrorists are just like enemy soldiers. They must expect to be treated harshly if captured by the enemy.

b. _____ Torture is justified in certain situations, for example, when a person who has placed a bomb on an airplane or in a crowded building refuses to tell anyone the details about it.

c. _____ Torture can never be justified under any circumstances.

d. _____ Torture is sometimes necessary to scare other potential terrorists from committing crimes.

e. _____ Once you torture one person for one reason, it becomes easier and easier to justify the use of torture for all sorts of reasons.

f. _____ Torture can make people admit to crimes they did not commit.

g. _____ Torture is necessary to maintain law and order.

h. _____ Only people who deserve to be tortured are tortured.

i. _____ Very few people actually get tortured. Just the threat of torture is enough to make most prisoners "talk."

# VI. Further Topics for Discussion and Composition

1. Can the use of torture be justified under any circumstances? Give examples to support your point of view.

2. Why do you think that international agreements such as the Universal Declaration of Human Rights do not prevent the widespread use of imprisonment and torture in the world?

3. Look at the cartoon by Colin Whitlock on the next page. Create a new caption for it.

4. a) A white dove in a dark jail cell is often used as a symbol for Amnesty International. Do you think this symbol is effective? Why or why not?

   b) Other Amnesty International symbols include a single lit candle entwined in barbed wire and a pen dipping into a bottle of blood-red ink. Design a poster for Amnesty International that uses these or other appropriate symbols.

*Canada and the Global Village*

Courtesy Amnesty International

Courtesy Amnesty International

Courtesy MacDonald and Co. (Publishers) Ltd.

# VII. Learning Log

Go back to your journal and spend the next few minutes recording what you have learned and experienced from this particular unit. You may use your first language if this helps you to better express more complex ideas or insights.

## Word List: Crossword Puzzle

| | | |
|---|---|---|
| ADOPTS | MALARIA | RECURRING |
| BITTERLY | MALNUTRITION | RESTORATION |
| CONSCIENCE | MIDWIFE | SET |
| DIPLOMATIC | NEUTRAL | SNIPERS |
| EROSION | OPPRESSIVE | TORTURE |
| FATE | PATROL | UNSANITARY |
| INTERPOSITION | POVERTY | VIOLATIONS |
| LITERACY | | |

# Crossword Puzzle

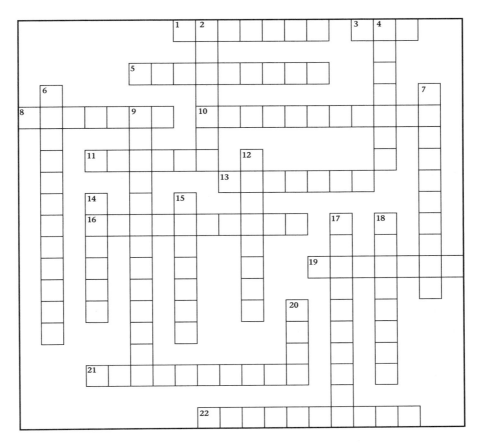

### Across

1. Peacekeepers are often fired upon by _____ .
3. Canada is governed by a clear _____ of democratic principles.
5. Some African countries suffer from _____ bouts of famine.
8. _____ is a disease passed by the bite of certain mosquitoes.
10. Land _____ is an important part of OXFAM'S work.
11. Canadian peacekeepers are often asked to _____ a country's borders.
13. A woman who helps another woman during childbirth is called a _____ .
16. Peacekeepers keep the peace while _____ solutions are found.
19. Many countries use _____ on political prisoners.
21. Prisoners of _____ are imprisoned because of their beliefs.
22. A lot of countries are ruled by cruel and _____ governments.

### Down

2. It is important that peacekeepers remain _____ in disputes.
4. Soil _____ can occur when trees in a certain area are cut down.
6. Not getting enough food to eat can lead to _____ .
7. Many children in the world live in extremely _____ conditions.
9. During the Suez Crisis, Canadians played an _____ role.
12. The two warlords fought _____ for control of the small country.
14. Amnesty _____ prisoners and works for their release.
15. Millions of people in the world are living in _____ .
17. Peacekeepers have to monitor cease-fire _____.
18. _____ programs help teach people to read and write.
20. Amnesty holds governments responsible for the _____ of prisoners.

# Notes

## Introduction

1. Linda Baker and Nancy Stein, "The Development of Prose Comprehension Skills," in C. Santa and B. Hayes, *Children's Prose Comprehension, Research and Practice* (Newark: International Reading Association, 1981), 7–43.

2. J. Cummins, 1979. "Linguistic Interdependence and Educational Development in Bilingual Children." *Review of Educational Research* 49:2, 222–251.

## Chapter I   Sun, Sea, Wind, and Sky

### I-1 Canada's Endangered Wilderness

1. *The State of Canada's Environment*, Government of Canada, Ministry of the Environment (Canada: Supply and Services Canada, 1991), 5–6.

2. Helen Caldicott, *If You Love this Planet: A Plan to Heal the Earth* (New York: W.W. Norton & Co., 1992), 53.

3. Paul McKay, "Is Canada declaring open season on northern wildlife sanctuaries?", *Toronto Star*, Nov. 29, 1990, A21.

4. David A. Gauthier and David Henry, "Misunderstanding the Prairies," *Endangered Spaces: The Future for Canada's Wilderness*, ed. Monte Hummel (Toronto: Key Porter Books, 1989), 91.

5. Glen Bohn, "Rare bird, mouse and rabbit found in Okanagan join endangered species list," *Vancouver Sun*, April 16, 1994, A4.

6. Dr. David Suzuki, forward to Michael M'Gonigle and Wendy Wickwire, *Stein: The Way of the River* (Vancouver: Talonbooks, 1988), 12.

7. Arlin Hackman, "Endangered Spaces: Ten Years for Wilderness in Canada," *Borealis* 1(4), 1990, 27.

8. Working For Wildlife Newsletter, Spring 1992, 4.

9. Mark Hume, "Poachers to be among targets of watch program," *Vancouver Sun*, Oct. 28, 1992, B6.

### I-2 Just Another Load of Garbage?

1. "Reduction and Reuse," Environment Canada Fact Sheet, June 1991.

2. Tom Rattray, "Demographics and Discards: Why there's more garbage, and why packaging isn't the culprit," *Garbage: The Practical Journal for the Environment*, Dec./Jan. 1993, 27.

3. "Solid Waste: Out of Sight, Out of Mind," *The State of Canada's Environment* (Ottawa, 1991), 25–26.

4. "Solid Waste," 25–29.

5. "Waste Management," *The Canadian Green Consumer Guide*, (Toronto: McClelland and Stewart, 1989), 103.

6. "Solid Waste," 25–26.

### I-3 Saving the World by Cycling

1. R.C. Mackenzie, "Have You Driven Forward Lately?", *Canada and the World*, March 1992, 18.

2. Ed Ayres, "Breaking Away," *World Watch*, Jan./Feb. 1993, 11.

3. Ayres, 14.

4. Ayres, 12.

5. "The Bicycle," *The Canadian Green Consumer Guide*, (Toronto: McClelland and Stewart, 1989), 124.

6. Ayres, 12.

7. "The Bicycle," 124.

8. Joel Makover, *The Green Commuter* (Bethesda, Maryland: Tilden Press, 1992), 7.

9. Tom Koch, "Bike to Work Week," *Pedal Magazine,* May 1992, 42.

10. Rick Milliken, "Can Bicycles Save the World?", personal essay, 2.

11. Mackenzie, 18.

12. "Cyclists Win Race For Time"

13. Ayres, 13.

14. *Perspectives on Labour and Income,* Statistics Canada, Summer 1994, Cat.# 75-001E, 18.

15. Robert Sarti, "City to give cyclists a smoother ride," *Vancouver Sun,* June 9, 1992, B4.

# Chapter II Toward a Healthier Canada

## II-1 Dr. Peter: AIDS Educator

1. *Quarterly Report,* Division of HIV/AIDS Epidemiology, Laboratory Centre For Disease Control, Health Canada, Oct. 93.

2. Christine Gorman, "Invincible AIDS," *Time,* Aug. 3, 1992, 18.

3. "What Causes Aids? A Second Look," *Ideas,* CBC Radio, Nov. 6, 7, 1991.

4. Peter Jepson-Young, "Dr. Peter," *Witness,* CBC Television, 1992 (Sept. 18, 1990, segment).

5. Jepson-Young (Dec. 7, 1990, segment)

6. Dr. Peter as quoted by Don De Gagne, "Sufferers urged to take lead in AIDS fight," *Vancouver Sun,* Nov. 30, 1992.

## II-2 Of Shamans, Plants, and Healing

1. W. Byard Roger, "Impressions of Folk Medicine in the Andes," *Canadian Family Physician,* Vol. 33: December 1987, 2815.

2. Stephen Fulder, *The Handbook of Complementary Medicine* (Britain: Coronet Books, 1989), 14.

3. Stephen Fulder, "Complementary medicine," UNESCO *Courier,* Aug. 1987, 19.

4. Kevin Barker, "Home Remedies," *Better Health,* Summer, 1992, 8.

5. Heidi Miller, "Some Quebec docs finding homeopathy a natural alternative," *Medical Post,* Sept. 29, 1992, 35.

6. Earl Mindell, *Earl Mindell's Herb Bible* (New York: Simon and Schuster/Fireside, 1992), 12.

7. Arnold and Connie Krochnal, *A Field Guide to Medicinal Plants* (New York: Times Books, 1984), 87.

8. Alma R. Hutchens, *Indian Herbology of North America* (Boston: Shambala Publications, 1973), 303–304.

9. Mindell, 13.

10. Mindell, 208.

11. Anne McIlroy, "Seeking wonder drugs among forest's secrets," *Montreal Gazette,* Feb. 16, 1991, J5.

12. Thomas Land, letter to the editor, *New Leader,* Nov. 17, 1986, 3.

13. John Noble Wilford, "Folk-remedy extract of ginkgo tree synthesized," *Montreal Gazette,* March 12, 1988, J14.

14. Todd Kimberley, "Drug claimed to halt tumors", *Vancouver Sun,* Feb. 1, 1993, A5.

15. Mindell, 248.

16. Mindell, 208.

## II-3 The Sounds of Silence

1. Leigh Silverman, "Earning a Deaf Ear: Loud Music and Hearing Loss," *Audio,* Jan. 1989, 76.

2. Marilyn Miller, audiologist, Workers' Compensation Board of British Columbia, interview, February 1993.

3. "Ping," *Sports Illustrated,* Aug. 6, 1990, 14.

4. Katherine Lanpher and Kathryn Keller, "Turn Down That Noise! Everyday sounds can cause hearing loss," *Redbook,* Apr. 1991, 58.

5. Kevin Krajick, "Loud But Not Clear," *New Choices for the Best Years,* Sept. 1990. 32.

6. Gary Graff, "Loud, Proud and Deaf," *Calgary Herald,* June 22, 1989, C1.

7. Krajick, 32.

8. Lanpher and Keller, 62.

9. Lanpher and Keller, 62.

10. "I Can't Believe What I'm Hearing: Noise Pollution," *Current Health,* Sept. 1990, 29.

11. Krajick, 35.

12. Mary Gooderham, "Environmental noise hazard takes heavy toll," *Globe and Mail,* Apr. 18, 1991, A7.

13. Gooderham, A1.

14. Krajick, 35.

# Chapter III Taking Action Against Crime

## III-1 High Tech Crime Fighting

1. Sandi Farran, "Artists age photos, rebuild faces to help police," *Toronto Star,* Sept. 6, 1992, B8.

2. Jon Zonderman, "High-Tech Crime Hunters," *Popular Mechanics,* Dec. 1991, 30.

3. Walter Buchignani, "Making Faces: Computer artist helps take a byte out of crime," *Montreal Gazette,* May 20, 1990, A4, A5.

4. Zonderman, 29–30.

5. Zonderman, 30.

6. Linda Pulak, "Genetic Sleuths," *Calgary Herald,* Aug. 15, 1992, B9.

7. Pulak, B9.

8. "The gene-pool police: Jasper wardens battle poaching with high tech," *Alberta Report,* Sept. 9, 1991, 24.

9. Tracie Cone, "Witness for the prosecution," *Montreal Gazette,* March 18, 1990, B9.

10. Cone, B9.

11. "Gunpowder Fingerprinting," *Popular Mechanics,* Oct. 1992, 28.

## III-2 These Hackers Don't Play Golf

1. John Greenwood, "Big hack attack: how hackers are costing business a bundle," *Metropolitan Toronto Business Journal,* April 1991, 28.

2. Greenwood, 30.

3. Bruce Sterling, *Hacker Crackdown: Law and Disorder on the Electronic Frontier* (New York: Bantam Books, 1992), 49.

4. Greenwood, 28.

5. Greenwood, 28.

6. Sterling, 59.

7. Ken Campbell, "The computer as professor of crime," *Globe and Mail,* Aug. 3, 1991, D3.

8. Sterling, 104.

9. Linda Marsa and Don Ray, "Crime Bytes Back," *Omni,* Aug. 1990, 100.

10. Paul Mungo and Bryan Clough, "The Bulgarian Connection," *Discover,* Feb. 1993, 56.

11. Greenwood, 27.

12. Greenwood, 30.

13. François Shalom, "Computer fraud grows in Quebec," *Montreal Gazette,* Nov. 7, 1990, G2.

14. Mary Pitzer, "Keyboard capers: Insiders seen as greatest threat," *Montreal Gazette,* Oct. 28, 1990, B8.

15. Sterling, 97.

16. Campbell, D3.

17. Carolyn Van Brussel, "Signed oaths best protection against crime, say expert," *Computing Canada*, July 4, 1991, 1, 7.

18. Greenwood, 154.

19. K.C. Toth, "Feds launch all-out assault in bid to cut crime," *Computing Canada*, Nov. 7, 1991, 46.

## III-3 Building Community Partnerships

1. Clare Lewis, Dr. Ralph Agard, and James Harding, *Report of the Race Relations and Policing Task Force*, Ontario, 1992. Report prepared for the Honourable A.C. Pilkey, Solicitor General of Ontario, 147.

2. Jean Leonard Elliot and Augie Fleras, *Unequal Relations: An Introduction to Race and Ethnic Dynamics in Canada* (Scarborough: Prentice-Hall Canada Inc., 1992), 251.

3. Kathryn E. Ashbury, *Building Police–Community Partnerships with Culturally, Racially and Linguistically Diverse Populations in Metropolitan Toronto*. Ontario Council on Race Relations and Policing, January 1, 1992, 10–12.

4. Stephen Lewis, letter to Premier Bob Rae of Ontario, June 9, 1992, 12.

5. John Demont, "Frustration in Blue," *Macleans*, Nov. 16, 1992, 21.

6. Chinatown Police Community Services Centre brochure

7. Lewis, 35.

# Chapter IV Protecting and Providing

## IV-1 Wronged and Rights

1. "Employment Agencies Raided," *Calgary Herald*, Feb. 1, 1991, A2

2. Ruth Teichroeb, "Racial discrimination adds to the torment of job search," *Winnipeg Free Press*, Sept. 9, 1992, B1.

3. Jane Armstrong, "Job-seekers facing silent discrimination," *Toronto Star*, Feb. 17, 1991, A1, A2.

4. *Harassment Casebook: Summaries of Selected Harassment Cases*, Canadian Human Rights Commission, 1991, 9–10.

5. Gordon Clark and Charlie Anderson, "Racism rap costs McDonald's $2000," *Vancouver Province*, Dec. 1991.

6. Virginia Galt, "Ministry inaction cited in harassment charges," *Globe and Mail*, May 15, 1991, A8.

7. Paula Guerette, "Racial Harassment," *Toronto Life*, Nov. 1991, 104.

8. Galt, A8.

9. Allan Gould, "Nobody's Puppet," *Toronto Life*, Nov. 1991, 104, 218, 220.

10. Radha Krishnan Thampi, "Harassed workers offered cash," *Winnipeg Free Press*, Oct. 6, 1990, 1, 4.

11. For an excellent guide on how to deal with racial harassment and violence, please see "How To Deal With Racial Violence," Canadian Antiracism Education and Research Society (CAERS), 10667–135A Street, Surrey, B.C., V3T 4E3.

## IV-2 In Service of Others:

1. Doreen Duchesne, *Giving Freely: Volunteers in Canada*, Statistics Canada Labour and Household Surveys Division, (Ottawa, 1989), 32.

## IV-3 Consumers Protected

1. *Consumer Karate: A defense manual for people who spend money*, Consumer Association of British Columbia, 1985, 71.

2. *Consumer Karate*, 71.

3. "Are you involved in a dispute?", information pamphlet by the Law Foundation of British Columbia.

4. "What is a BBB?", information brochure from the Canadian Council of Better Business Bureaus.

# Chapter V  Canada in the Global Village

## V-1  The Reconciliation: Canada's UN Peacekeepers

1. Dave Todd, "Keeping the Peace," *Canadian Geographic,* Nov./Dec. 1992, 56.

2. Todd, 59.

3. J.L. Granatstein, "Peacekeeping," *Canadian Encyclopedia,* 1634.

4. Department of National Defence, "Backgrounder: Canada's Contribution to International Peacekeeping," Dec. 1992, 1–4.

5. *Soldiers for Peace: Supplement to MHQ: The Quarterly Journal of Military History,* vol. 5 (1), Autumn 1992.

6. "Backgrounder," 1–4.

7. Tom Walton, "Clearing mines keeps Bombs R Us busy," *Vancouver Sun,* Nov. 10, 1992, A10.

8. Captain Ray Lalande, "Children of the Desert," in J.L. Granatstein et al, *Shadows of War, Faces of Peace: Canada's Peacekeepers* (Toronto: Key Porter Books, 1992), 40.

9. J.L. Granatstein and Douglas Lavender, "Cyprus," in *Shadows of War, Faces of Peace: Canada's Peacekeepers,* 44.

10. Granatstein and Lavender, 113.

11. Granatstein and Lavender, 89.

12. "Peacekeeping monument unveiled," *Vancouver Sun,* Oct. 9, 1992, A9.

## V-2  Helping People to Help Themselves: OXFAM Canada

1. Gary Bellamy, "Somalia isn't the only horror," *Globe and Mail,* Oct. 16, 1992, A25.

## V-3  Getting Away With Murder

1. "Letter Writing," *Human Rights Education, Amnesty,* International British Section, 1983, 4.